Growing up in the Okanagan

by

Vivian E. Merchant
Vernon, B.C., Canada

August 2017

GROWING UP IN THE OKANAGAN

Forward

This book *Growing up in the Okanagan* describes my experiences in growing up, to explain my life to my own children, to my many relatives, and to friends and associates. I believe that the Okanagan was a wonderful place to grow up in, and I want to describe what life was like here and the many factors that made it such a great place. The description of the many jobs that I've had while growing up and the jobs that my parents have give a greater sense of what life in the Okanagan was like.

This book contains two interconnected tales; the first is the story of my life which has not been ordinary, but exceptional. I had the privilege of being brought up living on the shores of Kalamalka Lake, in the Okanagan Valley, one of the most beautiful locations in Canada. My father was an avid and prolific photographer, so I can amply illustrate the story.

Accompanying my story and intertwined with it is the history of my parents Joe and Mary Merchant, who left England in the depression following the Second World War to seek opportunities in the new world. In my years as a young man, my life was inseparable from those of my parents. They initially suffered through temporary hardships upon moving from England, but within two years had their own house in Canada and in eight years lived beside the shores of Kalamalka Lake. Their path to success in the new world is a path that perhaps other immigrants could emulate.

Vivian Merchant
August 2017

Acknowledgements

The Author thanks his wife Michelle, his friends Bob and Joyce Hebbert and Terry Hurst and his sister Daphne Mackenzie for comments on the manuscript, which have lead to significant improvements. Many thanks are also given to the Vernon and District Museum and Archives for providing photographs for the book and the staff for encouragement in putting it together.

In photograph captions, the initials JWM indicate the photograph was likely taken by the author's father Joe Merchant. The initials VEM indicate the photograph was taken by the author. For a number of pictures, the photographer is unknown.

TABLE OF CONTENTS

Forward . . . . -ii-

Acknowledgements . . . . -iii-

TABLE OF CONTENTS . . . . -iv-

INTRODUCTION . . . . -1-
    How My Parents and I (at age 4) came to the Okanagan
    . . . . -2-
    The prehistory - My early days . . . . -3-
    The Migration . . . . -4-

OYAMA 1952 & 1953 . . . . -9-

SALMON ARM 1954 . . . . -16-

VERNON 1954-1959 . . . . -20-
    The Parent's Story . . . . -21-
    The first Canadian-owned home . . . . -23-
    The Neighbourhood . . . . -25-
    Life in Vernon . . . . -26-
    Schooling . . . . -26-
    Movie Evenings . . . . -30-
    Boyhood Activities . . . . -31-
    Summer Vacations at Pierre's Point . . . . -37-
    Summers at Okanagan Lake . . . . -39-

COLDSTREAM 1959-1965 . . . . -45-
    The Parent's Story . . . . -47-
    My Story Continues . . . . -49-
    Home Improvements . . . . -49-
    Radio and television in the home . . . . -52-

Expansion into the lake . . . . -54-
Cottages and Piers . . . . -56-
Life Beside the Lake . . . . -58-
Our Watercraft . . . . -62-
Exploring the Lake . . . . -69-
Aquatic and Shore Life . . . . -73-
Earning and Learning Experiences . . . . -74-
Dry-Land Boyhood Experiences . . . . -77-
Adventures in Ranching . . . . -84-
Summer Vacations . . . . -85-

JUNIOR HIGH SCHOOL - GRADES SEVEN TO NINE
. . . . -88-

THE HIGH SCHOOL YEARS . . . . -92-
Cars and Other Activities . . . . -99-
Summer Jobs . . . . -104-

LOOKING TO THE FUTURE . . . . -112-

CONCLUSION . . . . -115-

Figure 1 Map of the North Okanagan region, showing the main city Vernon, other places where the author lived (Oyama, Salmon Arm, and Kalamalka Lake) and the location of summer camps (Pierre's Point, Ewings Landing, and the Okanagan Indian Reserve).

GROWING UP IN THE OKANAGAN

INTRODUCTION

This is the history of a boy raised in the beautiful Okanagan valley in Western Canada, and of his parents who emigrated to the great unknown of the new world. I hope the story gives the reader a feeling of everyday life of a young boy, the influences on him as he was growing up, and some feel of what makes the Okanagan a special place. There have recently been magazine articles and television shows suggesting that the Okanagan is one of the best places in North America in which one can retire, because of the style of life and the weather. But it was also a great place to have been brought up. Here in the Okanagan, I grew up, went to school in Vernon, worked at a large variety of summer jobs that typified BC industry, and played in and on Kalamalka Lake. What Canadian boy ever had a better boyhood?

My siblings and I were fortunate to grow up not only in the Okanagan, but also to have lived for a number of years beside Kalamalka Lake, the "Lake of Many Colours", at a time when the lake was a "swimmer's lake". We took swimming classes at the public beach, and could swim from our home to the beach, and sometimes even swam across the lake. Occasionally people would swim in front of our house, going from residences farther up the lake to the public beach. There was an annual "Kal Lake Marathon", with swimmers going from Oyama to the public beach at the Vernon end of the lake, a distance of about 12 miles. The lake was beautifully clear, and one could see the bottom even at a great depth.

Now the lake has evolved to be a "power boater's lake". During the months of July and August there is a constant roar of powerboats from six-thirty in the morning till sunset. The lake is no longer beautifully clear, but is a mud slurry from the turbulence of the boat propellers. The water frequently tastes of gasoline, and is unpleasant to swim in.

One can no longer swim from the houses around the lake to the public beach; it is far too dangerous because of the high population of power boats. Being raised there now would not be the same experience, and we were lucky in the time period in which we grew up, that we had a "swimmer's lake".

I moved from the Okanagan to attend Simon Fraser University, when the University first opened in 1965. Starting at the latter university years, I returned to the Okanagan only for occasional vacations. I moved back in 2005 with my wife, and once again took up residence in Vernon. Some comments in this manuscript recognize the changes that took place in the North Okanagan between the time described in this book and the time that I returned.

How My Parents and I (at age 4) came to the Okanagan

I was born in England to parents who had just survived the terrors of the Second World War. During the war, my father had joined Britain's Royal Air Force, and was sent to Canada for training under the Commonwealth Air Training Program. He met some wonderful people in Canada who became lifelong friends, and they were somehow different from the people he had known in the industrial English town where he was raised. His early history and life in the air force is described in the book *Joe Merchant RAF*.

My mother was born in a depressed industrial town in the North of England, but she moved to the southern town of Grays, where opportunities were greater, in the mid 1930's. Her family background, upbringing, and early career is described in *Mary White from Ramsbottom*. Note that Mother had been a remarkably successful person in Grays. Working at the Thurrock Council, she was able to get a mortgage to purchase a home .... the number of single women purchasing homes at that time was infinitesimal, but our mother did it.

My father and mother met at a dine-and-dance banquet in which my father was playing the drums in the "Havana Dance Band". They were married in June of 1941, in a time period in which my father was employed at the Bata Shoe factory in Grays. After the excitement and camaraderie of the Air Force days during the war, Joe found it difficult to go back to the factory job that he had prior to the war and had when my parents met. Mother didn't understand him giving up this career, but Joe's sister thought it had been a miserable job with long hours. Joe wanted to be independent, to work for himself. They bought a store/dairy in Grays. Father bought bulk milk from farmers, rebottled it, and delivered it door-to-door with a horse-drawn wagon. The house that mother had purchased was sacrificed for this business venture; there was accommodation in apartments above the store. Father however made up his mind that Canada was the place to be.

During the war, he had met a gentleman named Harry Byatt, who described life in the Okanagan Valley, and how there were so many opportunities to make a living here. So the Merchants and the family of Mother's sister (the Claydens) packed up their possessions and moved to British Columbia, the western province of Canada. We don't know the details that persuaded the two families to move, but mother frequently spoke about Harry Byatt saying the streets were "paved with gold"

The prehistory - My early days in England

I was told that I had a speech impediment of some kind, and took speech therapy classes in England prior to the migration. I was adventuresome enough to ride a bike down the rockery stairs in the garden at the back of our house. We lived in the upstairs of a store for a while, and Mother reminded me of an occasion when my older brother Peter and I found our way into a jar of jam in the shop. My Uncle Gordon and his wife lived with us for a while, and I was captured on film smoking Uncle Gordon's (unlit) pipe.

Figure 2 Vivian and the rockery steps (JWM)

The Migration

In 1952, a migration from England to Canada took place, consisting of Joe and Mary Merchant and sons Peter (born 1946) and Vivian (born 1947) along with my mother's sister Nora Clayden, her husband Bill, and their son Brian (born 1946). We crossed the Atlantic Ocean on a Greek liner, the *S.S. Columbia*, leaving Southampton on July 12th, 1952; my "landed immigrant"

Figure 3. The SS Columbia preparing to leave for the new world, with the Clayden and Merchant families aboard. The picture was likely taken by an uncle that accompanied us to Southampton, from where the ship left England.

pass is stamped in Quebec City on July 21st 1952. Mother was apparently very sick on this journey; this was initially attributed to sea-sickness. It was later ascertained that she was pregnant with my younger sister Daphne during this voyage. Of the trip from England to Canada by boat and travelling across Canada by car, I have few memories. Strangely, I had remembered being taken care of during the boat trip by a young lady, and playing amongst the lifeboats with her. In discussions many years later, mother insisted that there was no other young lady (though mother was confined to her bunk most of the time because of the seasickness and morning sickness), except possibly a young girl a few years older than Peter and myself.

We travelled to Toronto, where we stayed for a little while with some people called the Kemps. My father, Joe Merchant, had first met them when he was in Canada training for the Royal Air Force. The Kemps become lifelong friends and visited us several times when we were established in the West.

Figure 4. Aboard the SS Columbia. Peter on the left, Vivian on the right and in the center an unidentified girl that stuck in my memory, but mother denied that she existed. (JWM)

Figure 5 A picnic while the two families crossed Canada in the 1947 Nash. Joe Merchant was likely taking the picture.

The two families purchased a five-year-old car, a 1947 Nash, and drove to the small village of Oyama, in Canada's western province of British Columbia (BC). The old Nash carried both families across the continent together. Somehow, four adults, three children, and all the luggage were squeezed into this car. My cousin Brian remembers sleeping in the corner of the back seat which was like a huge old sofa. My older brother Peter remembers sleeping across the front seat of the Nash during the trip across Canada; the parents may have slept in a tent. A lot of the roads were gravel, Brian remembers unpacking the trunk to get at the jack and the spare tire, and patching inner tubes. For myself and the other children, this was all a big adventure.

We crossed the Rocky Mountains at the Crows Nest Pass. After driving uphill for a long time, my brother Peter asked, "Is this where we see God?"

Part of our route across Canada went through the United States; this was considerably before the completion of the Trans-Canada highway.

OYAMA 1952 & 1953

Initial Hardships - There was unfortunate incidents in the life of young Vivian Merchant, and a period of hardship for the family upon arriving in the promised land.

Photograph of the isthmus of Oyama,
taken by Vivian Merchant
from the Campbell-Brown Nature Preserve.

Upon arrival in BC in early August, we first lived in Oyama, a small orchard community a few miles south of Vernon. The new immigrants had bought the promise that in BC the streets were "paved with gold" and full of opportunity, but found initially it was necessary to get menial jobs picking apples and maintenance work in the packing house to put food on the table. The economy of Oyama was entirely dependent on agriculture.

It was during the Oyama period that Daphne was born in the Vernon Jubilee Hospital. Our family met Harry Byatt and family upon first arriving in Oyama, as documented by the attached picture. My parents must have been sufficiently impressed with the help provided by the Byatt's that their new-born daughter was named Daphne after Harry Byatt's wife.

My parents quickly found that there were limited opportunities for people such as themselves without significant financial resources. When we first arrived in Oyama, one of Father's jobs was at the Fruit Union, sorting and boxing apples for shipping, but also doing maintenance work. The Fruit Union was a cooperative owned by a collection of orchardists, to collect the fruit from different orchards, inspect and grade it, prepare the fruit for shipping, negotiate rates with the railway company, and find markets for the fruit. The Fruit Union building, sometimes called the "Packing House", was adjacent to the railway tracks on the Oyama isthmus.

We lived in the Fruit Union building for a while, spending our first Christmas in Canada there. I remember being given a brightly coloured plastic toy tractor as a Christmas present at a community gathering. This was likely the only Christmas present I got that year. It was presented by a fellow dressed in a Santa Claus outfit. If there's anything I remember about him, it is that he was a particularly skinny Santa Claus. Maybe they were short of candidates for that year. Afterwards, when we went to bed, I left the Christmas present on the steam register beside my bed, and overnight the plastic melted. This was a great disaster for me, and

I cried for a week, but there was no replacement!

We moved from the fruit union to a house owned by a Mrs. Boucher, although I have no recollection of this. I do remember our next home, a "picker's shack" on the edge of an orchard. This is a rudimentary house meant for temporary labour hired to pick the fruit crop in the fall of the year; these people were migratory as they weren't need year-round.

In my memory, there was a big white impressive mansion at a distance in the middle of the orchard. I recently (65 years later) drove around Oyama and could find nothing that looked familiar, I couldn't find the spot where we had lived. This was near to some people called Thompson, who had children roughly our age.

Figure 7. Family picture in Oyama. Back row, right to left: Harry Byatt, Daphne Byatt, Mary Merchant, Joe Merchant, unknown but possibly Daphne's sister Verite. Front row, right to left, Peter Merchant, Susan Byatt, Vivian Merchant, possibly Sarah Byatt. Picture likely dates from the fall of 1952, after the Merchant's arrival in Oyama but before Daphne Merchant birth in March 1953.

What do we know about Harry Byatt, this mysterious man responsible for our family immigrating to Canada? I personally have no recollection of him. Joan Heriot describes returning from England to the Okanagan with Daphne Byatt, the daughter of a Coldstream farmer (no page number), in "Growing up on the Coldstream", A memoir Joan Heriot. (No publisher, printer, or year listed. Possibly 2004.) From the Heriot book: "In Canada, Daphne joined the Women's Army Corp (WAC) which was how she came to meet her future husband, Harry Byatt. Harry was a pilot in the RAF, training Canadian pilots here rather than in England, where things were more difficult. Just before their marriage in November 1944, Daphne's unit had a short spell of duty in England. .... After the war Daphne and Harry had a fruit farm at Oyama where I went for a visit in the summer of 1948. Their first daughter, Susan Ruth, born in 1946, was a lively toddler ..."

In the Vernon Museum and Archives, there's some archival pictures detailing Harry Byatt's contributions to farm irrigation in Oyama.

But we didn't play with them much, I believe because of the social differences between us, living in the shack, and them living in the big house. Imagine being conscious of social differences when only five years old. I think I must have learned this by osmosis from my mother who was ashamed of the circumstances in which we were living as compared to the comfortable house she had purchased in England, but which was sacrificed to my father's ambitions. Aunt Nora said that it was necessary to get water from a stream near this shack, carrying it in a bucket for household use, and that mother really hated this place.

I was involved in a car accident with mother when we lived in Oyama, as she drove the car off the road going up a hill in the winter snow. I got a cut on the forehead, and the scar was visible for many years afterwards. I wasn't badly hurt however, the main effect was that Mother became a very timid driver. Likely, she hadn't driven much prior to moving to Canada. Her sister, my Aunt Nora, never did learn to drive.

We did live in Oyama during the coronation of the Queen Elizabeth II. I have dim recollections of a big community picnic, and had a shiny teaspoon commemorating the coronation for many years, although I don't know what happened to it over the course

Figure 8. Playing in the water in Oyama, from left to right Brian Clayden, Peter Merchant, and Vivian Merchant. In the distance is the packing house where the Merchants lived for a while, and adjacent to that is the railway tracks on which trains carried the packed fruit to market towns. (JWM)

of time.

The best set of family friends from the Oyama period was a Scottish-Canadian family, Scotty and Frances Allen and their son Billy. They operated a small orchard of a few acres. None of the family were particularly talkative, but they became good friends of my parents and I believe helped us out in those dreary times. Scotty and his son ran the orchard, which consisted of apple and cherry trees; great big trees with huge spreading boughs that result in the whole orchard being shady. Because of the extensive

-13-

Figure 9 Peter and Vivian on the roof of the packing house in Oyama. The picture is labelled "Xmas 1952". (JWM)

irrigation the grass between the trees and was long and thick, and it was quite pleasantly cool between the trees even on very hot days. Irrigation water was brought to the orchard by wooden flumes; three pieces of wood arranged in a U-shape channel carried the water. This flume ran across the top edge of the property, which was on the side of a hill. The water was carried from the flume down the hill in metal tubes about three inches in diameter; the tubes had periodic sprinkler heads that spread the water in circular area around the sprinklers. I think they were run purely by the hydrostatic pressure of the water coming down the hill. The sprinklers had to be moved every few hours from between one row of trees to being between an adjacent row of trees. Because of the number of these pipes, moving them occupied a good fraction of the day for Scotty or Billy. And although he was only a few years older than Peter and myself, Billy Allen worked very hard on the orchard.

We stayed in touch with the Allen's for many years after. I worked one year picking their cherries. This was done on fourteen-foot-high, three-legged ladders. The picker had a large bag; it had canvas sides and a metal bottom, and was suspended by a strap around the picker's net. The canvas was sewn around a metal frame into a semicircular shape with rounded corners. With this on, he or she climbed the ladder, and pulled the cherries from the tree (with stalks attached), and placed them in the bag. When he had picked all the cherries within reach from the ladder, he would climb down and move the ladder to a new location, periodically emptying the bag of fruit into wooden apple boxes. This was done very gently by releasing the hinged metal bottom to the canvas bags, and letting the fruit flow into the box without bruising.

I was a very inefficient picker, preferring to eat the fruit rather than putting it in the canvas sack. But I was doing it as a favour for the Allens, who couldn't find pickers that year, rather than for money.

In 2006, when driving by the location of Scotty Allen's house and orchard, I noticed that the orchard had been torn up and replaced by a housing development.

SALMON ARM 1954

The family moved to Salmon Arm because of a job possibility for Joe Merchant, but the job didn't work out; subsequently he worked away from home. The remote jobs became a step towards a permanent job in Vernon.

Vivian Merchant started school.

The view from the home of Nora and Bill Clayden.
Photograph by Vivian Merchant.

The Parent's Story

Father had been promised a job in Salmon Arm, about fifty miles north of Oyama, so our family moved there in 1954. The job - perhaps with Okanagan Electric - didn't work out, and Dad didn't get paid for the work that he did there. Subsequently whenever we drove from Vernon to Salmon Arm, we were instructed to spit out of the window at a certain house - this was the home of the man who didn't pay Dad. Eventually and fortunately for this scoundrel, the road to Salmon Arm was rerouted and we no longer passed his house. Peter said that Dad worked at Okanagan Electric long enough to learn how to wire a house, a skill which was useful later.

My brother Peter believes that while in Salmon Arm, Dad had a job delivering coal for a few months.

While Dad was out of work, mother went out to work even though she was pregnant with my younger brother Richard. Dad did get a job with a logging company, operated by a relative of Harold Thompson, our neighbour in Oyama. These jobs were away from Salmon Arm, in Albert Canyon about a hundred miles to the north east, and later in Blue River a hundred and fifty miles to the north west. The job was with horses and not machinery. Dad said that everything went well as long as he did what the horses wanted. There was great excitement when he returned home for weekends after working away. Both of the areas where he worked have a much greater annual rainfall than the relatively dry Okanagan Valley, and the forest grow very thickly.

Our father worked in a rough-and-tumble logging camp, a very different environment from where he came from in England. In the logging camp, he handled the horses that hauled the big logs from where they were cut to the nearest road from where they could be extracted by truck ... and he got this job because he had handled horses as a dairyman in England.

I can only imagine his thoughts as he lay in his bunk at the logging camp, what have I got myself and my family into? He was no doubt the highest educated man at the camp, having a diploma from Palmer's Boys School. But the camp was only a step along the way. But from contacts made at the logging camp, he got a job with a company in Vernon BC (J.S. Galbraiths and Sons) that supplied equipment to the logging camps. A Galbraith's worker named Tony Cope, who later became a foreman at Galbraith, came to Salmon Arm with a truck and helped move us and our possessions to Vernon.

Because father used the car to get to his remote job-sites, Mother used to have to walk around the sprawling village. She walked through heavy snowfall to the place she worked on the far side of the village. At one point she was being driven home, and on the way up a steep hill, her door of the car came open and she

Figure 11 Daphne, Vivian, and Peter on the steps to the verandah in the house in Salmon Arm. (JWM)

flew out landing in the dirt. After Richard was born, she developed a persistent red rash, which Richard later called "Stevens Johnston Syndrome". In addition to these problems she had an 18-month old baby (Daphne), two active young sons, and an absent husband. In general, the Salmon Arm life was not good for our mother. She must have thought back on her time in England where she was able to purchase her own house.

The house where we lived in Salmon Arm had a great verandah extending around several sides of the house. This was before the days of air conditioning; people use to sit on lounge chairs on the shaded verandahs to cool off. The verandah with its white sides became our play area. There were some neighbours, Glen Philips and his wife, Mother said took care of us while she was working and in hospital for Richard's birth. At one point Mr. Philips had shot an owl, so we were all called out to have a look at this owl.

In 2006, I had occasion to drive around Salmon Arm with my Aunt Nora. She was able to point out the locale where we had lived, but I saw nothing familiar about the house at that location.

I started attending school in Salmon Arm; I have a vague recollection of a big room full of children, and one child in particular who was bigger than the rest of us. He was a native, and frequently used to wet his pants, which led to his being teased by the other children and the teacher had to assert her discipline. I felt sorry for him; it certainly wasn't anything that he could control.

VERNON 1954-1959

The family buys their first Canadian house - it requires a lot of fixing up, but it's a step forward.
Summer vacations at lakeshore cottages bond the family together.

The city of Vernon, nestled between the Okanagan hills
Photograph by Vivian Merchant, from the top of Middleton
Mountain.

The Parent's Story

We moved to Vernon when I was part way through my second year of school. This was in late 1954, Richard thinks a month or two after he was born in August. Dad had got a job with J.S. Galbraith & Sons, a Vernon-based International Harvester dealer and repair shop. In the late 1960s the company was bought by an Eastern Canadian conglomerate, and was closed down after in a few years after Dad had retired. The company sold and serviced crawler tractors and other heavy equipment primarily to the logging industry, one of the main industries in British Columbia.

The big crawler tractors were used in the forest, constructing roads to allow the big logging trucks to get close to the areas in which the trees were being fallen. The tractors were also used to haul the fallen trees from the locations in which they were first felled to the location in which they were loaded onto the trucks. The logs were cut to length to be loaded on the logging trucks, the eighty-foot (about twenty meter) length being the maximum that was allowed on the public highways. The truck drivers would have to be skilled at driving not only on the highways but also on the narrow purpose-built roads winding up the sides of mountains. These roads (on which no automobile could ever travel) had been put in place by the heavy-duty crawler tractors from companies like J.S. Galbraith & Sons.

The company's service area extended from the Kootenays to Prince George, about a quarter of the province of British Columbia. The heavy duty mechanics doing service work on the products put a lot of miles on their service trucks; at that time an average car would be used for eight to ten thousand miles per year, but the service trucks were driven ten times that amount each year due to the company's wide service area. The mechanics would repair a tractor in the forest work-site if possible, or if not possible would arrange for it to be hauled back to the Vernon shop.

Dad worked, not in the field, but in the two Vernon offices of the company. Once he got this job, he never left it for the rest of his working career. Mother said that he got the job because somebody in the company was a Mason; Dad and his father before him were members of the Masonic organization. An alternate explanation is that Dad got the job because he impressed the Galbraith service personnel that he met while he was working in the logging camps.

My brother Peter thinks Dad's first job at J.S. Galbraith & Sons was as a janitor. At Galbraith's, it was discovered that Dad was skillful at splicing wire rope. Wire rope is very important in the logging industry (to the point that one of Canada's biggest logging companies MacMillan Bloedel had a sister company Canada Wire and Rope to supply the logging operations) and was an expendable item that would wear out due to the rough usage. I remember as a youngster visiting Galbraiths after school and

Figure 13. The "yard" at Galbraith's and Sons, showing machinery waiting to be repaired, with Clarence Fulton Senior Secondary School in the background. Picture courtesy of the Greater Vernon Museum and Archives.

watching Dad doing the splicing. A final part of the splicing operation was pouring molten zinc over the spliced ends; the zinc would solidify and seal the ends.

At some point father became a bookkeeper, keeping track of how much time and what parts were used on individual repair jobs. Later he worked in the parts department, keeping track of the tool and parts usage on each jobs.

In my high school years I used to walk through the shop and watch the mechanics working on the big diesel engines that had been removed from the machines and placed on pallets. Other jobs they did included welding on the frames of the machines, with sparks flying in every direction.

The first Canadian-owned home

When we moved to Vernon, my parents were able to purchase a house in what was at that time a new part of town. The house at 2104 45th Avenue was only partly finished however, and not habitable. We lived in the garage at the side of the main house during the first winter while Dad fixed the house up to the point it could be occupied, including the first winter.

We had no extra money to hire carpenters to finish the house, so Dad did a lot of work to fix it up, in his "spare" time. Dad laid an oak floor that Mom thought was a major extravagance in the lounge. It didn't seem to be too long until we were living in the house, rather than the garage. I'm sure that for us little tykes, living in the crowded conditions in the garage was a lot of fun, but for our mother it must have been a terrible time.

Our house on 45th Avenue had a sawdust furnace, which was fed by a large hopper full of sawdust. The hopper had to be periodically refilled with sawdust, but it was not easy for Peter and I to reach high enough to do it. When Dad wasn't home, we had to fill a can with sawdust, climb up on a chair, and pour the sawdust into the hopper; it took a lot of child-sized buckets to fill that hopper. The force of gravity carried the sawdust to the narrow exit to the hopper, where it entered the fire. It was very

Figure 14 The home on Vernon's 45th Avenue. A great deal of work had to be done on this house, but it was the first house owned in Canada. To the right of the picture is the garage in which we lived until the house was habitable. (JWM)

important to make sure the hopper never got empty, or the fire would go out. It was quite difficult to get the fire going again once it went out; that was an adult job, not a child's job.

The sawdust was a waste product from local lumber mills, and was delivered periodically to the house. A whole room in the basement was devoted to storing the sawdust which was unloaded from the delivery truck through a window to the basement storage room.

In the house, Peter and I shared a room in the basement, it had very cheap fibreboard walls and we punched through these when we were rough-housing. Peter broke his bed bouncing on it one day. At one point we had visiting school students from Lewiston Idaho staying with us for a few days while they played in a band concert at the local school. I still have the little souvenir box they left as a memento.

Father and Mother were later able to sell this house at a considerable profit, although they personally carried a mortgage from the buyers.

The Neighbourhood

Mother was not initially comfortable in the neighbourhood largely populated by German and Ukrainian immigrants, although she became lifelong friends with some of them. Only a few years previously, mother's English neighbourhood was being frequently bombed by the Germans; now she had Germans as neighbours. The family did make friends with two English families, Thomas and Amy Hammond who lived several blocks to the north-west with their children Christine, Bob, and Roland, and Bill and Edna Renshaw who lived several blocks to the north east with their children Laurette and Cheryl. I remember going over to the Hammonds' home to watch a weekly television show "Zorro" on Saturday Morning, but I also remember listening to "The Scarlet Pimpernel" and "The Lone Ranger" on the radio in our living room. This was before the day of "superheros" who had unbelievable and unrealistic superpowers. In the shows that we watched, the heros were talented horsemen who wore costumes or disguises when they were in action.

As mentioned above, we lived in a neighbourhood with many people of European origin. A German family lived next door. They had a son named Oley, who had a hole in his heart (likely in the septum dividing the two chambers of the heart). Years later, Mom and Dad hired this German-Canadian fellow to do some carpentry at the house at the lake. Mother and Father also became friends with a Dutch family the Roelfsemas, who had a son nicknamed Dicky who was about Richard's age. They stayed for a while in the garage adjacent to our house after we had moved into the house itself. We didn't see much of them after we moved down to the lake; I believe they moved to a different town about the same time as our move. Mother used to say that my young brother Richard was a very well behaved little boy when by himself, but when he and Dicky got together they were holy terrors and got into all kinds of trouble.

Life in Vernon

A small dog called Smokey was added to our family when we lived at this Vernon house. Smokey enjoyed biting the postmen's legs, and before too long the postal service stopped delivering mail to us. My parents had to collect our mail at the downtown post office.

The first car in which we had driven across Canada was superceded by a newer and smaller Nash station wagon when we lived on 45th Avenue.

While we lived there, I had a bunch of teeth extracted, which entailed an overnight in the hospital; this must have been expensive for my parents. The intent was to extract one of the adult teeth in each quadrant of the mouth to ensure there was enough space for all the adult teeth as they grew in. All the extractions were done in one operation, instead of multiple operations. This operation was not un-common at the time, but later was replaced by orthopedics using braces to correct the mouth by forcing the teeth to grow straight and evenly. The one-shot operation that I had was a cheaper alternative in the long run, and is now regaining popularity.

We were taught to cycle on the grass of Harwood school. One of Peter's first bicycles was an olive green paratrooper's bike; this is intended to be folded in half to be more convenient in size to carry while parachuting. Although it was meant for tough soldiers, Peter repeatedly broke the frame and Dad had to take it to his work to get it welded up.

Schooling

The back of the house was adjacent to the grounds of Harwood School. It was at this school that I took most of grade two (having started in Salmon Arm) and grade three, and on these school grounds where we played on Saturday. I remember learning to write with pens with nibs; each desk had a bottle of ink into which the nib was dipped. The nib was a bent and carefully shaped piece of metal that would hold a small amount of ink long enough for the student to transfer it to the exercise book, and practice his writing. What a revolution ball-point pens produced! No more ink bottles, no more pens and nibs, no more accidents with ink getting on the clothes or being spilled on the exercise books.

Since Harwood School only took students of grade one, two and three, Peter and I took grade four, five, and six at Beairsto

Figure 15 My father and his children on the grounds of Harwood school. I am to the left. (JWM)

Elementary School. We used to ride our bicycles the fifteen blocks to school, and sometimes go down to Dad's work after school. Occasionally Dad driving us and neighbourhood children to Beairsto school in the Nash station wagon. I had a teacher called Mr. Clark in Grade four or five, who gave us exercise after exercise on the multiplication tables, and grilled us endlessly. I disliked him at the time, but we really did learn our arithmetic very well.

One popular spring time activity at Beairsto Elementary School was marbles. Many of the boys and a few of the girls would have collections of marbles - round pieces of glass, some with a butterfly pattern inside, and some clear. A student would draw two lines in the dirt and set up one or more marbles in a line or in a pattern near one of the lines in the dirt. Other students would stand behind the second line and shoot the marbles at the one set up by the first student. If the marble that was shot missed those set up by the first student, that marble then belonged to the first student. If the marble that was shot hit one of those set up by the first student, all the marbles became the property of the student doing the shooting. The object of the game, whether the student was one doing the shooting or one setting up the marbles, was to get as many marbles as possible.

The student setting up the marbles had a challenge to attract students to try and shoot for his marbles; if he made the setup too difficult by making the lines too far apart or was on a rough stretch of ground, the shooters would just go elsewhere.

So the students would save their pocket money, buy marbles at the corner store and proceed to lose them in the game, while others would accumulate a huge stock of marbles.

One necessary part of the game was a bag to carry the marbles in; often one just used the bag that they came in from the store, but then you couldn't accumulate too many. The most prestigious bags were the purple cloth bags in which an expensive brand of whisky called "Crown Royal" came, but very few of the students had these bags.

We went to the Anglican church. I don't remember mother and dad going, but I do remember them driving Peter and me and picking us up afterwards. We were in the main service for part of the time, but then went into the Sunday school. I remember a Sunday school play in which I was the baby Jesus and had to lie in the cradle, but I must have been too old for that position. I was embarrassed because I wore pajamas in the cradle (didn't one always wear pajamas when you went to bed) but there was really nowhere to change into and out of the pajamas. I was glad when that play was over. We never went to Sunday school or church once we had moved out to the lake. The last time I was at church

Figure 16 Father and Richard, at the home on 45th Avenue in Vernon

I fainted because my tie was too tight, and my parents were called to the Sunday school to rescue us. But the knowledge that I'd picked up in those early Sunday School years stuck with me, and came back to me when I resumed going to church as a mid-thirty year old.

In that time period, our family had Bill and Edna Renshaw and family over to our house on Christmas Day, and went to their house on Boxing day (or vice versa) to prolong the celebration. These were always very happy times. For my parents, it was a link to the English culture that they had left behind.

Movie Evenings

When we were children living in the 45th Avenue house, we didn't have a television in the house. These were the early days of television broadcasts. Dad had seen television in England before moving to Canada and wasn't impressed with it. As an alternative, the parents and a group of their friends would have an occasional movie night. Movies and a sixteen mm projector would be borrowed from the public library. These were mostly travel and history movies. My father or Mr. Renshaw would run the projector. Present were the English ex-patriots that my parents met when they first moved to Vernon, Bill and Edna Renshaw and their daughters and Edna's father Mr. Philips. Mr. Philips was retired, but he had worked with Edwin Shaw, a nom-de-plume of Thomas Edward Lawrence, known as Lawrence of Arabia. Lawrence was hiding from all the publicity that had been brought down on him. Mr. Philips was convinced that Lawrence was not killed in an accident on his motorcycle, but deliberately killed by British Intelligence because of his Nazi sympathies.

Other participants at the movie nights included Tip and Amy Hammond, and a Mr. and Mrs. Wilson who had a daughter Karen. Sometimes these evenings would involve a game such as Charades, with both adults and children participating, when the movies were done. I also remember an occasional guest Harry Marshal, who had been in Burma and had movies of the elephants in Burma. The elephants were used in the Burmese logging operations. The site for the movie evenings would rotate from one house to the other, amongst the participants. I remember in the evenings when the movies were shown at the Wilson house, we children would disappear as Karen had a passion for playing an innocent game of "Doctors and Nurses". I wonder if Karen became a nurse when she grew up.

Boyhood Activities
The neighbourhood friends I had at the time included William, Bobby, and Ralph. Ralph had an accident with

Figure 17 Learning how to fix bicycle tires. Picture by JWM or possibly mother.

firecrackers, with a number of them exploding in his pocket, which meant a trip to hospital. Apparently I got in a fight with our neighbour's son, Bobby, and ferociously fought him off. I forget totally what we were fighting about, but mother reminded me many times about that fight. William lived across the street, and I think had a younger sister. On rainy days, we played board-games such as "Clue" on their living room floor, and I remember that he had a large set of a construction toy called "Tinkertoys". He went not only to the normal school, but to Ukrainian school on Saturday morning, to remain proficient in the Ukrainian language.

At that age, playing with girls was not on our agenda, or at best any occasions in which it did occur have not stuck in my memory. Thomas Hammond played cricket, and Peter and I occasionally went to the cricket pitch with him and his boys. In later years we joined and played on the cricket team, but just as fielders; we weren't old enough for any other roles. The cricket pitch was on the grounds of a private school in the Coldstream, The Mackie School. The cricket pitch is now a field, but the hut where the players rested when not playing still exists, although in a dilapidated state.

The group of neighbourhood boys used the grounds of Harwood School as our own personal territory. This is before the days when children had to be micro-managed, and were able to make their own fun. We played scrub softball, not usually with teams. Another game was *Red Rover*, where the participants were in two lines, holding hands. One fellow was called "Red Rover, Red Rover, will Peter come over"; the person called had to run across the gap and try and break through the line of the opposing team-members. If he broke through he returned to his own line, but if he didn't break through, he joined that line. We spent many Saturdays doing this.

Near where we lived there was a somewhat older boy named MacDonald who had what seemed to be an enormous paper route. We used to see him occasionally with the papers piled high on the carrier in the front of his bicycle. My memories may be a bit distorted ... he wasn't a full grown young man yet, so the size of the pile of papers must be considered against the height of the boy. Because of his paper route, he was the "richest" kid on the block, and was able to build motor-driven model aeroplanes as a result of his hard work. Some of the planes he would fly on control lines in the school ground. They made enough noise that whenever he started them up, he would quickly get an audience of youngsters standing, watching, trying to help. Others he would just let "free fly". They would circle upwards, and drift off into whatever direction the wind was blowing. Then this large crowd of youngsters would chase the airplane until it came to the ground several blocks away. This chase would mean running down streets, cutting through yards and fields, climbing over fences, doing whatever it takes to keep up with the airplane moving high overhead. We were likely a great nuisance to the homeowners, but it was all tremendous fun. We looked forward to the days when he would let a plane go in free flight. But he didn't do this too often, as they inevitably ended up damaged. The planes actually only flew a few city blocks, but it seemed like a foreign adventure to a six year old.

Somewhat to the north of us was a gravel pit, that had enormous piles of sand and gravel. A group of us young boys would climb to the top of the gravel heaps, and tumble all the way to the bottom, getting sand incorporated into every item of our clothing. This was huge fun for us youngsters, but probably not appreciated by the workers. Walking through the fields on the outskirts of town, we used to find garter snakes, grab them by the tail and whirl them around our heads and then release them to fly.

There was a forestry Entymology department in the woods to the west of our house. The occupants studied the interaction of the various types of insects with the forests that provided the wealth of the land. These labs were wooden frame building with white shiplap siding; as of this time of writing there is no trace left of the buildings. I remember one of the workers taking me inside and showing me the large collection of bugs and moths there, each one neatly labelled and pinned to a backboard. I started my own bug collection after that; I remember my parents bought me some carbon tetrachloride to kill the insects.

In the summer, Peter and I and perhaps some of the neighbourhood boys would ride our bikes to Kalamalka Lake to go swimming. I imagine that we did this while Mother and Father were at work; I can't remember what happened to the younger children; they must have had a babysitter or somebody looking after them. This was a long bicycle ride for eleven and twelve year olds, all the way across the big city of Vernon, and then down the long winding road to the lake. The road didn't have a paved shoulder and we would have to get off the road onto the dirt adjacent to the pavement whenever a car was coming. The large public beach at the lake had dingy changing rooms, which were later torn down. There were several lifeguards along the length of the beach, who used to sit on big white stands. I don't think they ever had to rescue anybody, but they kept order on the beach. We didn't really know how to swim at this time, except what our father had taught us, but we were there just for the fun, anyway.

Peter and I were (for a while) members of the Junior Forest Wardens; I still have their manual and I still can't identify different tree species. The Junior Forest Wardens were an alternative to the Boy Scouts; they were founded because the forest industry was so important to the economy of Canada. I don't remember how we came to be involved, but we were driven to evening meetings in the cafeteria in the basement of Beairsto school. I can still get a mental image of all these boys with red uniforms with white lanyards over the shoulder playing amongst the big wooden tables in the cafeteria. When we moved to the home at the lake, it was too much trouble to go to town for evening meetings and this got dropped.

It was while living at the Vernon house that I started stamp collecting. I remember trading some old Canadian stamps that I had come across to another young collector, and later regretting

Figure 18 Peter as a Junior Forest Warden, with the 45th Avenue house in the background. (JWM)

this trade. I used to buy bags of a thousand unsorted stamps and spend considerable time sorting them out into their respective countries and time periods. This became a lifelong habit, and for many years I had a superior knowledge of the geography of the world, what countries were called, their history and major events, all of which was attributed to stamp collecting. The hobby was perhaps ruined by the many countries who saw issuing stamps as a source of revenue, and pumped out great quantities of stamps that were not relevant to their culture or history. My great feat as a stamp collector was finding an old Hungarian stamp with a spelling error on it. My parents encouraged me to write to one of the stamp magazines, Stanley Gibbons in England, who then ran an article saying "a 12-year-old Canadian collector has found an error ...." At that time, only two other copies of stamp with the error had been found. Mother did everything she could to help me; she had heard that stamps postmarked on their first day of issue, if kept on the original envelopes, were especially valuable, so I have some stamps in my collection on company envelopes from her employer at the time. But I also have stamps on envelopes from locations where members of her family were working, in Malta and Australia.

One of my first jobs was selling seeds. I had a catalogue from the seed company, and went around door-to-door asking people what type of seeds they would like. The order was sent into the seed company, and when the seeds arrived, I delivered them to the homes that had ordered them. I forget at what point the money was collected ... this job must have been when I was eleven years old or younger, because it was when we lived in the house in town. This type of job existed because most homes had only a single car at that time period, and usually the main wage earner used that car for transportation to and from his work. The majority of wives stayed home, and had no way to go shopping during midweek. Moreover, this was before the era in which the forty-hour work week became standard. Many men worked a 48 hour work week, and my father worked a 44-hour work week (half day Saturdays). When father came home from work on Saturday, mother and father used to go to the grocery store to do the week's shopping. Items such as bread and milk were delivered to the homes by bread vans and milk men that had assigned schedules. The lack of opportunities to go shopping led to the job that I had selling seeds. Many households that had only one wage-earner had substantial gardens that provided a significant amount of food. Some households even kept chickens for the supply of eggs, although this was contrary to the city by-laws. Preserving fruit and vegetables for winter meals was very common in this time period (late 1950's); most households had "canning" sessions in the fall. Today, home preserving is very much a lost art.

Another job that Peter and I had when we lived at this address was at a chicken farm. Mother or dad drove us to the farm, and then picked us up afterwards, so it was probably as much trouble for them as the money we earned. Peter, who had the job first, remembers riding his bicycle to the chicken farm and back with another neighbourhood boy. This collection of boys had to go into a yard that was full of chickens, grab some of them by the legs, and throw them into baskets. At this point I forget what criteria was used to decide what chickens were selected for the basket, but they didn't like it. The chickens used to fight back, of course, and I remember having a multitude of scratches on my arms and legs.

Summer Vacations at Pierre's Point

In the years before we went travelling on our summer

Figure 19 Peter (front) and Vivian playing on air mattresses at Pierre's Point, near Salmon Arm. (JWM)

vacations, we rented lakeshore cabins for a couple of weeks each summer. These vacations were initially at Pierre's Point on Shuswap Lake, then at Ewing's Landing, and finally we camped on leased land on the Indian Reserve on the west side of Okanagan Lake. These were very carefree days, spending all day on the beach, sometimes reading, sometimes making rafts out of any available logs, sometimes playing in the sand. I remember having a huge appetite for reading, and soaking up the books by authors such as Enid Blyton. I read every book by this author in the school library at Beairsto school, and got very involved in stories of the "Famous Five" and the "Secret Seven".

The family went for a number of years to Pierre's Point for summer holidays. We stayed in a very crude wooden shack, without insulation and I think without even electricity. The room was lit by a gas light, and cooking was on a wood stove or a Coleman gas stove. But what carefree days! We spent the time either reading, walking the beach, making rafts out of stray logs, or just exploring. The sandy beach seemed to extend for miles, at least a little child's miles. Behind the cabins was a huge thick forest, and we found sawn-off stumps of trees so huge that one could hide in the interior rotted part of the stump. Also in these forests were hazelnut trees, from which we would collect and feast on the hazelnuts.

In my mind we went to Pierre's Point for extensive periods, but I don't think this could have been so since Father only had limited time periods when he could have got off work. I remember the very large variation in the water height of the lake. In the earlier part of the year, the water was very high with the lakeshore being very near to the cabins. But by the end of August the lake level had considerably receded, and there was a very extensive beach between the cabins and the lakeshore. To observe this, we must have been at the lake in different seasons.

Behind the cabins, there was a very short stretch of woods, a fence and then the rail tracks. These weren't just ordinary rail tracks, but the main rail line between eastern Canada and the west coast seaport of Vancouver. Several times each day enormous trains used to pass by. For the kids it was another great game, counting how many cars there were on each train, and how many engines. There was frequently more than a hundred cars on the train, and up to seven engines.

Summers at Okanagan Lake

As the years passed, instead of going to Pierre's Point, we went for a couple of years to a crude cabin at Ewings Landing on the west side of Okanagan Lake. There was a very small cabin here and an outdoor toilet, but not much else. The disadvantage is that the beach here was very rocky, as a contrast to the beach at Pierre's Point. Adjacent to us was another property occupied by a family called the Barons. Mr. Baron was a manager of one of

Figure 20 My younger brother and sister, on a home-made raft. (JWM)

the banks in Vernon. He had a son called Tony who became a good friend to Peter, who was the same age. They also had a daughter who was about the same age as I was, but whom we seldom saw, and a younger daughter. Ewings Landing had its name because, prior to the days of road transport, the main system of transportation was by steamboat along the length of Okanagan Lake. The boats steamed between the city of Penticton and Okanagan Landing adjacent to Vernon, stopping at a number of places, called "landings" down the lakes. Ewing's Landing was one of these places where the boat landed. An early settler wrote[*], "Even in winter, our transportation was provided by the paddle wheelers on the lake. We would go down to our wharf and flag the *Aberdeen*. The good old paddle-wheeler made the trip up and down the lake once a week, and was the main source of delivery for home supplies. If the lake was too stormy for a landing, we went without our mail and food supplies until the next trip."

In the years in which we holidayed there, the dock constructed of enormous timbers to which the steamboat was tied was still there, but the boats had long since been replaced by rail and road. When we stayed at Ewings Landing, this abandoned dock was one of our main play areas. At one point, Tony Baron, Peter, and I were fishing off the dock. Our father was not a fisherman, so we had no knowledge to guide us on good fishing techniques. We were using whatever fishing gear could be scrounged or inexpensively purchased. My fishing career ended when Tony Baron, while casting with a three-barbed hooked, accidentally caught my brother Peter. Two of the three barbs of the hook were buried deep within his skin, and it took a lot of careful manoeuvring by a frantic neighbour to extract the barbed hooks. After the years in which we spent our summer holidays at Ewings Landing, there were a few years in which our summer holidays

---

[*]"The Leckie-Ewing Story", by Eleanora
(Ewing) Heal, in Okanagan History, the 59th Report of the
Okanagan Historical Society, (1995)

Figure 21 The SS Sicamous stern-wheeler pulling into the wharf at Ewing's Landing. The stern wheelers were no longer in service when we stayed at Ewing's Landing. (Photo 11339 courtesy of the Vernon and District Museum and Archives).

were spent on a beach lot leased from an Indian band, a few miles north of Ewings Landing but also on the west side of Okanagan Lake. When the Europeans first occupied the western part of North America, vast tracts of land were set aside by treaty as "Indian Reserves" for the aboriginals to preserve their traditional way of life, living off the land by farming, hunting and fishing. But many of the aboriginals, including those in the Okanagan, have found a far better way of life comes from the money found by leasing the portion of the Indian land immediately adjacent to lakes and rivers.

For at least a couple of years, our family leased a plot of lakeshore land on an Indian reserve. I don't recall that our plot had a cabin at all; we must have slept in a tent during the time we stayed there. But it did have an outside toilet, or "biffy". We didn't make friends with the children at any of the neighbouring campsites. This location had a sandy beach, as distinct from the rocky beach at Ewing's landing, so this was a huge improvement.

I remember one evening when we were enjoying a campfire on the beach, there was a party of young people at a neighbouring campsite. We could hear them swimming, and it was obvious from the conversation that they were skinny-dipping, that is, swimming without swimsuits. Once they were in the water, without their suits on, our playful father threw a huge pile of logs on the fire, so it blazed ferociously and lit up the beach for a considerable distance. The swimmers were too embarrassed to emerge from the water.

The land on which we stayed was the end unit of a number of lots leased from the Indians on the reserve. Immediately adjacent to the lot leased by our parents was a swampy area and beyond that was a pier used for log dumping by logging companies. Huge logging trucks holding many tons of logs would drive out on this pier. The restraining poles on the side of the truck would be removed, and the logs would pour off the truck into the water adjacent to the pier, causing an enormous splash. On one occasion, this was captured on movie film by our father.

A log boom surrounded the pier, consisting of a number of logs tied together by chains. The log boom formed an enclosure preventing the logs dumped into the lake from the logging trucks

Figure 22 Log boom used to store and accumulate logs until there was a sufficient amount to by hauled to the saw mill. The outer logs were chained end-to-end and served to retain the loose-floating logs inside. (VEM)

from floating away. When the log boom was full and couldn't hold any more logs, it was towed by tug boat to another location on the lake where there was a sawmill where the logs could be sawn into lumber more useful for construction.

The log booms were big enough that they only needed to be towed once every week or more. In the meanwhile, the logs were constrained by the log boom but available for children such as my brother and myself to play on. Dressed in bathing suits, we used to run from one end of a log to the other, trying to get all the way down the log before it started rolling. If the log rolled, the runner would inevitably end up in the water beside the log, or worse trapped between two logs. There were also huge pilings to which the log booms were secured. We would climb to the top of these pilings, and dive into the water.

From our leased plot of land, the road down the west side of the lake could be seen, but it was separated from our lakeshore camp by a field of tall wild grass. In accessing the leased lots, one drove down the road past most of the lots before turning off the main road into the side road leading to the leased land. One day, when we were expecting my aunt, uncle, and family from Salmon Arm to visit us, Peter saw them approaching along the road, and went running across the grass field to show or tell them the way.

Figure 23 A 2011 photograph of the remnants of the huge pier that had held the weight of a fully-loaded logging truck, a pier to which the logging booms were attached fifty years previously. (Photograph by VEM)

But in the grass there was concealed a barbed wire fence into which he ran at considerable speed, causing significant scrapes from the barbs in the wire. It took a lot of band-aids to heal him up; Dad had an impressive knowledge of first aid, and kept a large first-aid-kit in the car when we travelled. With three active young boys, he had ample opportunity to use this knowledge.

COLDSTREAM 1959-1965

The Family purchases a home at Kalamalka Lake.
Vivian and siblings enjoy the lake.

The District of Coldstream surrounding Lake Kalamalka.
Photograph by Vivian Merchant in 1969, from the highway
viewpoint overlooking at the lake. In the following years, many
of the orchards were pulled out and replaced by housing.

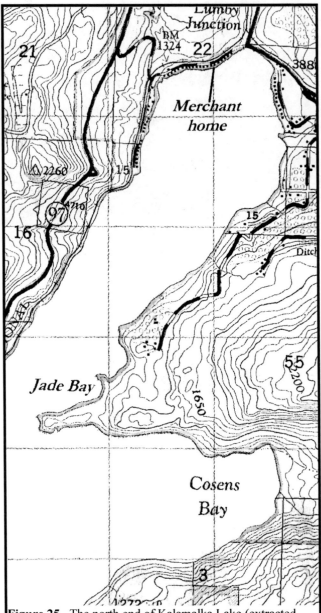

Figure 25. The north end of Kalamalka Lake (extracted from Topographical map produced in 1961, the approximate location of the Merchant home is indicated.)

Figure 26. The family (minus Dad, the photographer) at the Kalamalka Lake house. From left to right, Richard, Vivian, Mother, Peter, and Daphne. The beach on which we were standing was later surrounded by a concrete wall and filled in to extend the lawn area. (JWM)

The Parent's Story

When I was half-way through Grade VI the family moved to our Kalamalka Lake house (1960). The main house on half the lot was purchased, and sometime later when they could afford it Dad and Mom purchased the second half of the lot which held two rudimentary cabins.

My father remained working at J.S. Galbraith and Sons, as he did for the rest of his working career (even when the company was sold and took a new name). My mother had a sequence of jobs, and memory does not allow placing a time period for the various jobs or even our place of residence. An early job was at McDowell Motors, an automobile dealer in Vernon. She later worked for the gas company Inland Natural Gas at a time period in which Natural Gas (i.e., methane) was being introduced as a fuel for heating of homes and hot water tanks. It replaced coal and wood burning which left soot and ashes that had to be cleaned up and coating chimneys that subsequently had to be cleaned. Natural gas, the clean fuel, did not have these disadvantages. She made friends at the natural gas company with two families, the Cottrells and the McGraths, who became friends of our family.

Later my mother worked at E.B. Cousins, a notary public that also sold insurance. Here she learned the details of doing real estate transactions such as registering the change of ownership. This knowledge was a big boost when she later became a real estate agent.

My mother also worked at a government office, that of the health unit that monitored and administered the public health of the area. Her superior was Dr. Duncan Black, who had been captured by the Japanese when they conquered Singapore in early 1942. He spent the rest of the Second World War in a Japanese Prisoner of War camp, and his health was seriously compromised. He was an alcoholic who kept a bottle in his desk at the Health Unit, but apparently perfectly capable of doing the work. Although we didn't hear many details, there was a lot of petty infighting amongst the staff members of the health unit. Mother became friends with a number of the staff, however, and met with many of them socially at square dancing and other activities.

One of my dominant memories of this time period was my mother complaining nightly repeatedly that she wanted to go home, "home"meaning England. This seemed to be a persistent non-ending topic. It must have been very frustrating and aggravating for father to hear this time and time again, but he never reacted. It was only after her first trip back to England (late 1960's) that mother admitted that she had found that "home" was in Canada. But for years it seemed she was unhappy in Canada and was here only because her husband, encouraged by that rapscallion Harry Byatt, had dragged her to Canada. I remember hearing about the mysterious Harry Byatt and his "streets paved with gold" many, many times.

In this time period, my parents became more active in the community. They not only became very involved with square dancing but were on the executive of the Square Dance club. My father was on the Board of the local Credit Union, master of the Masonic Lodge, and founder of a corp of Navy League Cadets for training school age children in the naval arts.

My Story Continues

We lived at this lakeshore home for five-and-a-half years before Peter and I left to go to University in Vancouver, and this time period has become a huge part of the memories of growing up. As our parents continued to live there for years afterward, the Kalamalka Lake house has became fixed in memory as the family home, with the other residences merely steps along the way. These were the years in which I attended junior high school at what is now the W.L. Seaton School and senior high school at the Clarence Fulton Senior Secondary School in Polson Park.

Home Improvements

The house we moved into had initially been just a summer cabin, owned by the grandfather of one of my school friends. It had a coal-burning furnace installed to heat the house and to make it habitable in the winter. One room was devoted to storage of coal.

While we were living there, the family did a tremendous amount of hard work in improving the house and property. The banks between the house and the road were just sloping ground, dirt covered with bushes. These were replaced with concrete walls. A load of gravel was delivered to our parking space beside the road. Dad would buy bags of concrete, and mix it in with the gravel and water, either by hand or with an electric mixer. Peter and I carried bucket after bucket of concrete down the stairs, and poured the concrete from the buckets into frames. The lower two terraces were built with rocks from the lake added to the concrete

Figure 27 Improvements on the lakeshore home. This picture shows the lawn in front of the house being extended into the lake, with a concrete retaining wall and much dirt being imported to fill the ground inside the wall. Also shown is the shade being built in front of the house, to protect against the hot Okanagan sun. One of the boats is turned up for winter storage. (JWM)

to make a rock wall; the hope was to use up all the rocks and make a sandy beach. This however made only a small dint in the rocks in the lake, and resulted in a rock wall that didn't look too great. Thereafter Dad and Mother came up with some pink granite rocks, and the upper steps in the terraced wall looked considerably more professional. The wall is shown in figure 42 in the last chapter.

The house had no basement, but did have a dirt crawl-space underneath the floor joists that supported the living space. A big hole was dug in the dirt crawl-space underneath the house, to a depth below the water level of the lake. Dad did all the digging, and passed out buckets of dirt, that Peter and I had to dispose of. The hole was then lined with special waterproof concrete; this meant carrying more buckets of concrete down the stairs. The original coal furnace was removed from the house, and a new oil-burning furnace placed in the concrete-lined-hole in the crawl space under the house. The furnace heated water which was pumped to radiators in every room of the house. Dad plumbed in waterlines though the entire crawl space under the house to carry the water to the radiators. That was a hellish task as there was less than two feet of room and he had to move on the knees and elbows with the head down, to avoid bumping on the floor joists.

Special hydraulic circuits were installed so the same hot water furnace heated the water for the domestic uses. A pressurized water reservoir was installed so the furnace could draw on hot water as needed. A sump pump was installed so the concrete pit could be kept free of seepage, as it was below lake-level. All this was engineered by my father, but executed with help from his two older boys.

When this was done, the coal storage area was enlarged so the two bedroom house became a three bedroom house. Initially, the two younger children Daphne and Richard occupied the bedroom that used to be the coal storage room. Daphne had a very tall bed with storage space upstairs; she had to pull open the drawers to simulate stairs that she could use to get into bed. The two older boys slept in another bedroom which also had two desks for them to do homework and studying. In later years, the three boys slept in the same bedroom, with younger Richard in the top bunk of a set of bunk beds and Peter in the lower bunk. I was in another tall bed made from a door, with storage space underneath it.

The location of the original coal furnace was walled in to produce an entrance foyer, with closet space. The rest of this area was converted to a storage area which later contained a deep freeze to allow Mother to buy food in bulk. This kept food costs under control in a house with teen-agers with enormous appetites. An example of the frugal living was the consumption of "day-old" bread at a cost of fifteen loaves for one dollar.

The home improvements didn't stop there. Dad dug out the septic system, and refurbished it. Part of the yard was just unfinished dirt. Father and his boys hauled many pads of grass from a building site in downtown Vernon. A building was being expanded over an area that had been grass, and there was excess sod available. Daphne remembers helping to cut out the turf. We carried the sod down the stairs, and laid the sod on the area destined to become lawn. Father engineered a way to slide the sod down the stairs on the metal sides from an old washing machine, suspended from a pulley, using guy-wires to keep the rate of descent under control.

Radio and television in the home

Near my feet there was a jog in the wall and the adjacent area became a shelf on which I had a radio. This was a short-wave radio, and I would try and get stations from around the world, an activity called "DXing"*. I would listen to the BBC from London, Radio Cuba, and the US Armed Forces Radio network from San Mateo California, broadcasting to the American troops around the world. But it was the AM band where the radio really shone. It would pull in KGO, with Myer Bloom, a talk show host broadcasting from the "Hungry Eye" nightclub in San Francisco; KSL in Saint Louis, and a New Orleans radio station. My favourite station was KRED in Eureka California, because of its choice of music, with KRKO in Everett Washington being a close

---

* This must seem very primitive in the day and age of the internet.

second. And on Saturday nights there was Fraser McPherson being broadcast on CBC radio from the ballroom of the Hotel Vancouver. Earlier in the evening I listened to Hockey Night in Canada, and heard of the exploits of Boom-boom Geoffrion, the "Pocket Rocket" Henri Richard, Frank Mahovolich, and Bobby Hull. This was when the National Hockey League had only six teams. I listened to National Hockey League games on the radio for a long time before I saw my first game on Television or my first live game.

One magazine, "the Radio and Television Experimenter", carried a section called "White's Radio Log" which listed stations that could be heard far away, and their broadcasting frequencies. I used this as a guide to help identify the stations that I were able to pull in, based on the station's wavelength.

I took the radio apart a number of times as the tubes aged and had to be replaced, and this led me to taking a correspondence course in "Radio and Electronics" in Grade Eleven, as an option. The course briefly mentioned new-fangled things called "transistors", but was basically about the operation of vacuum tubes. The knowledge from this courses proved very handy later in my career when I was designing high power lasers using tubes to switch very high currents, much higher than could be handled by semi-conductor devices.

At the end of the bed, I had a small desk, and here I spent many hours doing homework and reviewing the day's school notes every evening. Although we had a television at this time of our life, Mother and Father had a policy that the television was not turned on during school nights. There was no cable, a set of aerials attached to the television pulled in signals from Vernon's broadcast tower. Once or twice however, our local station faded away, and we were able to pick up a fuzzy signal from a station in Eureka California. This signal must have taken a strong bounce in the ionosphere to reach us, as television broadcasts are at a high frequency that is usually not transmitted longer than 50 kilometers.

Expansion into the lake

There were concrete walls separating the grassy area from the lake. In some areas these walls were in poor condition, and were crumbling. The walls in these areas were knocked down and replaced; in the course of replacing the walls, they were relocated somewhat farther into the lake. Plywood forms were erected, and Peter and I carried a huge number of buckets of wet concrete mix down the stairs, and poured it between the forms. The forms did not make a tight seal with the lake bottom, and some of the concrete inevitably flowed out under the forms, producing a wider than necessary base. This situation was partly corrected by filling burlap sacks with a dry concrete mix, and lowering them in the water to form the lower level of the wall. Water would penetrate through the sack material causing the concrete mixture to turn into hard concrete. The cloth material would eventually rot away. The upper layers would be formed by pouring in buckets of concrete. Dad had bought some steel reinforcement rods, and these were incorporated into the wall. In places the weight of the concrete would cause the plywood forms to bell outward, so the walls were not always a uniform thickness.

After the walls were built, Peter and I had to carry a huge amount of dirt and fill materials down the stairs to bring the garden up to a level height. Then lawn was planted; after our first effort at moving the sod, our parents decided that it was easier to carry grass seed down the stairs than the heavy sod; one simply needed the patience while the seed was germinating and growing. The effect of all this work was that the size of the property had increased. And the local government was not necessarily aware of the increase.

But the overwhelming power of water and ice in wearing down concrete was not anticipated; in fact the walls in front of the

Figure 28. The process of repairing retaining walls, separating the land from the lake. This picture was taken years after most of the events in this book, and shows my sister Daphne's son Joel and husband Tom at work, repairing a concrete retaining wall. No earlier pictures of this work are available. (VEM)

house had to be repaired and rebuilt several times. A tremendous amount of work! Of course the two oldest boys Peter and Vivian were willing conscripts to aid in all this work. The immense willow tree that is currently in front of the house was started as a little twig from a willow tree in a neighbour's yard. The original tree is long since gone, but the one planted in the Merchant property lives on.

At one point, Dad had rigged a pulley system, so that buckets of wet cement, or dirt for the fill, could be more easily brought down from the road level to the level of the construction project. Peter or I would be at the top, and would lower the bucket on the pulley gently down to a lower level. The other one of us, on the bottom level, would remove the bucket from the rope, empty it into the frames, and replace it on the rope so it could be returned to the top for refill. If the person at the top wasn't too firm on the rope, the bucket would go racing down on the pulley and go crashing into the tree at the bottom. This happened once or twice, but we learned quickly.

Building these cement walls was not only hard work, but was also hot work. We frequently went swimming in the lake to cool off.

Sometimes the ebb and flow of the water in stormy weather would find holes underneath the walls. Then the dirt on the inside of the wall would be sucked into the lake. When this happened, one would see a huge area of muddy water flowing downstream from the damage spot, and eventually the ground would collapse into the cavity left by the dirt that was sucked into the lake. The soil would then have to be moved away to expose the bare concrete and the rocks underneath, and concrete repairs performed.

Virtually every house along the lake front was building walls into the lake, reclaiming land from the lake, and all were having the same problems.

Cottages and Piers

Immediately adjacent to our house were two primitive

summer cottages that were part of the parcel of land that Mother and Father had purchased. The cottages were sometimes rented out in the summer when we were being raised. One of the cottages was rented out year-after-year to a Mr. Gilbert and his family. The renters of the other cottage included friends who needed a temporary home, to a dentist who was in Vernon for the summer working at the Army camp in Vernon, and to a group of Calgarian friends who came summer after summer in later years. Although it was never mentioned, I imagine that the extra money from renting these cottages out was needed to supplement the family income.

Years later in Edmonton, I worked with a gentleman whose wife was the daughter of the dentist who inhabited the cottage while working in the summer at Vernon's army camp. In the 1990s I made business contact with a fellow working for a company in the Vancouver suburbs who had stayed in the cottage thirty years previously.

Both of the cottages had a short pier going out into the lake. Most of the other homes and cottages at the lake also had piers; the purpose is to allow mooring a boat avoiding the possibility that the motor or propellor would contact the lake bottom. These piers would suffer under the rough water and waves. The constant battering would knock the planks off the top of the piers, requiring frequent repair work. Worse than the waves was the winter ice. In some years the ice would get very thick, we frequently went skating in front of our house in the winter, and when I got my driver's licence I drove my parents car on the ice on the lake. But sometimes, particularly in the spring when the ice was melting but nevertheless still thick, the ice would move and carry everything with it. The posts that held the pier into the lake bottom would be twisted sideways by the moving ice, and the pier would have to be rebuilt when the water got warmer. Eventually, we gave up on the pier at one of the two cabins, and dismantled it.

In more recent years, piers are built which can survive year-after-year. This is partly due to the practice of pile-driving; there is now a commercial pile driver on the lake. When I was young nobody could have afforded to use a pile-driver, but as lakeshore properties have escalated in value, people with a higher level of disposable income have taken up residence. The pile driver uses the force of a falling anvil to drive a thick post of wood a couple of meters into the ground, and the ice cannot move the wood. The second reason why piers are now more stable is because the winters have got milder; as of the time of writing it is a number of years since the lake has had significant ice.

This construction work, the fun in the water, and the interactions with our mother and father contributed tremendously to our growing up experiences. Moreover, we learned from our father not to be afraid of any project. If something had to be soldered into place, fire up the torch and learn how to solder. If a pump had to be wired in, learn how to wire. Don't let any lack of knowledge stop you from getting the job done. We had a great and patient teacher in my father, but I think he had learned how to do it all himself.

After all the children had left home, the cottages were torn down and replaced with a newer permanent home.

Life Beside the Lake

My brother and I grew up as "part fish", we were in the water so much. I had joked that we put our bathing suits on when we got out of school in June, and took them off again when we went back to school in September, and I don't think this joke is too far from the truth. We were totally comfortable with being in or on the water.

At one point mother decided to learn how to golf, obtained some used golf clubs at a rummage sale, and got some used and chipped balls from the driving range. She wanted Dad to put some holes in the lawn for golfing, but these holes never came into being. We boys used to take the golf clubs and hit the balls as far as possible out into the lake. Then we went swimming to find the balls! The balls were usually in water that was over our head, but we had a fairly good recovery rate. But mother had a poinsettia plant that she had been given one Christmas, and she put the pot outside to enjoy the warm Okanagan sunshine. The plant had a long thin stem with a tuft of leaves at the top. An avid golfer-to-be took aim at the tuft of leaves on the top of the stem, and the poinsettia plant never looked as good again, with just a stem and no leaves.

We always took swimming lessons at the public beach. At that time, the pier at the public beach had a tower at the end, with two levels of deck and a diving board from each level. The diving boards were roughly at one meter, three and a half meters, and six meters from the water. I could dive off the second diving board, but don't think I was ever brave enough to dive off the top board. Even the second board would result in a painful head if one didn't hold the hands exactly right. I did however jump off the highest board. In diving off the second board, one could go down as far as the bottom if one tried, but it took an extra effort and the bottom was soft and muddy in any case. With the exception of the swimming lessons described later, all this activity was totally unsupervised as often many of the parents were working. In all the time I spent at the beach there were no accidents. Now the diving towers have been torn down for fear of accidents, and any diving from the pier is prohibited. It is likely not as much fun being a boy as it was in those days.

Close to the end of the pier, there was a set of long floating rafts moored in an L-shape, so the farthest part of the rafts were parallel to the pier. This is where swimming lessons took place, with swimmers going from the pier to the raft and back again, driven by the ruthless fierce swimming teachers. These "ruthless fierce swimming teachers" were high school students working at a summer job, but to us small boys they had many of the characteristics of Attila the Hun. How many times back and forth could a young boy do, particularly when this ruthless exercise was accompanied by criticism of the swimming style? It was instruction, not criticism, but the difference was minor when you'd rather be having fun than repeatedly doing lengths. But we went back year after year to this heartless torture, and became much better persons as a result of it. Years later, the swimming lessons at the public beach were stopped when an indoor pool was built in the city. My first exposure to swimming in chlorinated water occurred when I was twenty years old at Simon Fraser University.

We used to spend hours on the water on air mattresses and rubber tubes, and our skin assumed a dark brown colour. This was before the days when the effect of ultraviolet on the skin was of any concern, and we paid no regard to the amount of sunlight that we got. Because Dad worked at a tractor repair shop, he could get very large tubes (used and patched) which became part of the lake-side fun kit. We used to swim to and from the public beach, a distance of about a quarter mile, or paddle there on the air mattresses. Occasionally we used to swim right across the lake.

Later on, we became avid water-skiers. But this is left for a later section.

We discovered an abandoned car chassis a considerable distance into the lake, at the maximum depth to which we could dive. The chassis was clearly visible, as were piles of rocks in the muddy bottom. It is likely that the local residents would clear their beaches of rocks to try and generate a sandy shoreline by throwing the rocks on a raft, hauling them some distance into the lake, and dumping them. But the car chassis was our prize; it was an old car, and had wooden spokes. We used to dream of raising the car chassis, but never did. The water was so deep that our time-at-bottom was too limited to secure a rope to any part of the car. In recent years, the summer lake water is too muddy to find this car chassis, but it is still there.

One of our neighbours had a pier extending into the lake, although they didn't have a powerboat, and had a diving board on the end of the pier. Their son, Glenn, was about the same age as my younger brother Richard, but we all used their diving board in the summer months. My father used his eight-mm movie camera to take pictures of his four children diving into the water.

We did not spend much time fishing, although we did spend some money on child's fishing gear and play at it occasionally. One of our neighbours, a retired couple called Langstaff used to go down the lake about twice a week in their boat, either Mr. and Mrs. Langstaff together, or Mr. Langstaff with his two black Labrador dogs. We used to fish a bit from our shoreline, but rarely saw trout of any size. More often we saw suckers creeping along the shoreline, or occasionally a huge carp. Our end of the

Figure 29 Richard in the small boat. At this time, the boat had a small 1.5 horsepower gasoline motor. (JWM)

lake had a sandy or muddy bottom, without any features in the bottom that would encourage fish to live there. Further down the lake the shoreline was rocky and had many little bays and inlets more suitable for fish habitat.

Our Watercraft

Anytime there were two logs in the lake, there was a way to attach the two logs together and make a raft. Shortly after we moved to the lake, Peter was given an eight foot (two meter) long clinker-built boat by our neighbour. He experimented with a wide variety of sails for propulsion, after adding a cross beam in the boat to hold the mast. During this time, Dad acquired a 1.5 horsepower outboard motor, which we used on the boat for local exploration. For one reason or another, this boat was known as my older brother Peter's boat; perhaps it was originally given to him.

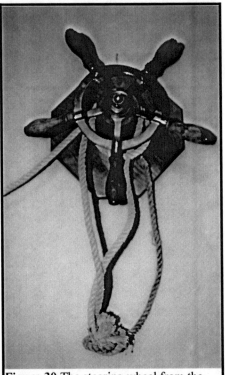

Figure 30 The steering wheel from the boat, presented to the Greater Vernon Museum and Archives. The rope is a later addition. (VEM)

Later, there was a longer boat that we were given from the man who used one of the neighbouring summer cabins, a Mr. Gilbert. It was perhaps 4 or 5 meters in length. We sailed this boat everywhere down the lake. It was a tremendous challenge to keep

Figure 31. The boat cut in half. It could be temporarily "fitted" together, and paddled for some distance. In the background is the pontoon raft with an ancient small outboard engine attached. (JWM)

these old clinker-boats free from leaks, or to keep bailing them when they did leak. Father had acquired an ancient 9.5 horsepower outboard motor which we used on this boat. It was very good experience for my brother Peter and me to experiment with these primitive outboard motors. To start the motors, a cord had to be wound around a pulley on the top of the motor, and rapidly pulled to cause the pulley and the motor to spin. If it didn't work, the process would be repeated with perhaps a minor adjustment of the throttle or choke position, until eventually the motor started. Pulling on the starter cord was hard work, however, and we both learned to start engines quickly.

We also learned about cotter pins and shear pins, safety mechanisms designed to protect the engines if the propellor hit a hard object such as an underground rock. If one of these broke while one was near the shoreline, one could leap out of the boat, stand knee-deep in the water, remove the protective cap from the propellor, and find and replace the damaged part. But if one was

Figure 32 The SS Sicamous, now on a beach in Penticton and turned into a museum.   (VEM)

in the middle of the lake when the damage happened, the repair person would have to precariously lean over the back of the boat to dismantle the propellor. The cotter and shear pins were designed to protect against solid objects, but sometimes would be snapped by the water pressure upon sudden acceleration. We learned to carry spare pins, and to do this repair. Today the widespread use of fluid clutches has lessened the possibility of shock to the boat motor's power train.

The leaks in this boat eventually made the larger boat not useful. We cut it across the centerline, and filmed a sequence where Peter in the rear and I in the front were paddling along and the boat fell apart. The remnants of the boat were scrapped. But I kept the steering wheel from the front of the boat, which had never been used while we owned it since the power motor at the back required too much personal attention. From discussions with Mr. Gilbert, we found out that the boat had originally been a lifeboat on the paddle-wheeler S.S. Sicamous, now a museum on the beach in Penticton. Prior to the extensive network of roads in the province, the SS Sicamous and similar boats on other lakes were a primary means of transportation to remote communities. In 2006, I presented the steering wheel to the Vernon and District

Museum, which had an exhibit on Okanagan boats.

The family went through several iterations of anchored rafts and powered rafts. The rafts provided a place to climb out of the water and rest, to dive from, and a source of transportation by poling or paddling. We had a five meter long tapered pole that likely started its life as a boat mast; it was useful for poling the rafts. The earliest rafts were made from logs, cut to the same length, with a planking on top to stand on. The planking was nailed to the logs and served to bind them together. But sometimes in severe storms one of the logs would come loose, and gradually the logs would get water-logged and want to sink and drag the raft down with them. So the wooden rafts would only last a season or two. The logs were mostly "found" logs that came drifting in, so they were probably half waterlogged to begin with. The most successful raft was one that Dad had made by welding together metal cylinders from sheet metal; this was done by one of the mechanics at J.S. Galbraith & Sons where Dad worked. The two long metal cylinders, ten or twelve feet long and painted bright orange, were joined together with lumber that formed a deck. With the ancient 9.5-horsepower outboard motor, this pontoon boat took us boys well down the lake past Cosens Bay. But most often it was anchored in front of our home, some distance off the shore, to prevent the powerboats from endangering swimmers by skimming too close to the shore line.

One of our favourite spots was a bay that was called "Jade Bay" or sometimes just "Second Bay". It was a considerable distance down a point that projected into the lake, dividing the lake into two arms. The point was always called "Rattlesnake Point", but the official name is really "Turtlehead Point" and the real Rattlesnake Point is further south on Kalamalka Lake. By the turn of the century, the city has grown to become quite close to this Jade Bay, and only the declaration of this land as parkland has stopped the development of this beautiful site. It had an isolated sandy beach on which we could pull up our pontoon boat. But more often, we would leave the raft out deep in this beautiful clear bay, and dive to the bottom to explore the plants that grew in the mud.

This pontoon boat eventually died, and another raft was made that lasted a number of years. This used large blocks of styrofoam packing material, restrained within the confines of a wooden frame and decking. There might have been two of these rafts, one of which disintegrated, and the lessons from the first one were used to build a second one which lasted for years. This raft was not meant to be mobile but just to be anchored in front of the house.

The rafts were anchored to a heavy concrete block fifty feet or so out from the shore, where the water was about four feet deep. This served well most of the time. But Kalamalka Lake could blow up very stormy at times. This made for very exciting swimming, going far out into the lake with the whitecaps, struggling with waves that seemed so huge. But the waves were not good for the rafts. The waves would lift the raft while the chain to the anchor was stretched taut, and the raft would lift the anchor and deposit it a few inches down the lake. The effect of many waves would move the raft into the neighbour's property. When the water became calm again, it was quite an exercise to get the raft back again. Several boys would get on one side of the raft, so that it sank partly under the water. We would attach the chain from the anchor so that it was taut with the sunken side of the raft. Then the boys would move to the other side of the raft, so the other side floated on the water surface and lifted the anchor off the lake-bottom. Then the boys would pole the raft back to its initial location, and finally drop the anchor back to the bottom.

Occasionally more serious problems would occur. The action of the waves would cause the metal links of the chain to chafe and wear, and occasionally the big waves would cause a link to break. Then the raft would go floating down the lake and be washed ashore on somebody else's property. This would require a boat trip to rescue the raft, once the water became calmer. But once the raft could not be found at all. Although most home owners were good about returning other's property, as the storm can cause damage to everybody, one unscrupulous person must have disguised our raft so that it was unrecognizable; and we never found it again.

In the first few years that we lived at the lake, there was no extra money to purchase a boat. Dad and his sons made a fourteen-foot "run-about" from plywood. Although it was usual at the time to apply a coating of Fiberglass to wooden boats for sealant and strength, this one was covered with a newer material called Celastic, which was introduced as an alternative to Fiberglass. This boat was powered with a used 30-horsepower Evinrude outboard engine, and was used to teach us how to water-ski. In fact this boat would pull two skiers; horses must have been a lot stronger in those days because now it seems to take a 200-horsepower motor to water-ski.

We learned to ski with two skis, which provided a lot of support; as we gained experience we graduated onto a single slalom ski. The single ski had a much deeper keel and consequently could be steered much more readily. I did not have a good enough sense of balance to start on one ski, but would start on two skis and kick one of them off after having gone four or five meters. Then the abandoned ski was close enough to shore that it could be recovered easily. When skiing, I would start from a sitting position on a pier. At the end of a run as the boat was approaching the starting point I would stay on the opposite side of the boat from the shore. As the end point neared, I would whip from one side of the other, which would dramatically increase the speed to twice the speed of the boat itself, and let go of the rope. With the extra speed, I was able to ski in to shore, losing speed and sinking into the water where the water was only shin deep. I was very proud of this ability to go skiing without getting the bathing suit wet. My biggest problem was my need for fairly powerful glasses, which I did not wear when water skiing, so that I had only a blurry view of everything that was happening. This was before the age of wetsuits, which would have been regarded as sissy stuff in any case.

We did have some spectacular "wipe outs" while waterskiing, which sometimes led to some painful injuries, but we were young and active and healed quickly.

Terry Dyck, another young fellow whose parents lived across the lake, had saved his money and bought his own boat. It was a small fiberglass boat, possibly ten feet long, powered by an eighteen horse power motor. This could pull a water skier, and would struggle with two skiers, so during the summer we would have endless fun in the water. With our boat, initially we would use it only on weekends, when dad was home from work, but before too long he trusted us with it by ourselves.

Father would buy gasoline in 45-gallon (200-liter) drums; this was less expensive gas than that used for automobiles because "road tax" hadn't been applied to it. It was a major challenge to lower a filled 45-gallon drum of gasoline down the slopes from the road level to the lake level. The drum was rolled down the hill in a rope sling, with a lot of boy-power holding the ropes at the top and gradually lowering it. The drums were then raised off the ground on a wooden platform, and a spout installed so that the boat's gasoline tanks could be easily filled. One drum would usually last more than one summer. This gasoline was a

Figure 33 The plywood boat, with left-to-right Vivian, cousin Brian, and Peter. This boat with the used 35 horsepower outboard motor would pull a waterskier. (JWM)

wonderful present from a father to his sons.

The celastic-covered plywood boat lasted until after Peter and I moved to the Vancouver area to go to University. The thirty-horsepower motor was too powerful for the plywood construction of the boat, and the stern to which the motor would be attached was coming loose from the rest of the structure, a very unsafe situation. An aluminum boat was purchased, which was powered by a brand new 7.5- horsepower outboard engine that mother had won as a door prize at an event. It had enough power to pull small children on tubes or air mattresses, or to go for a tour around the lake, but had insufficient power for waterskiing.

Most people who lived beside the lake had a boat. One of our neighbours, Jack and Edith Halverson, had a beautiful boat made of polished mahogany. Mr. Halverson worked at an Allis Chambers dealer, which was a competitor to the heavy equipment company that my father worked for, so there was a lot of friendly rivalry and joking. The two families shared not only the boating but also other activities such as square dancing.

Exploring the Lake

Kalamalka Lake is about twelve miles (20 km) long, extending from the public beach near Vernon to the community of Oyama where we lived when we first moved to Canada. The main feature of Oyama is an isthmus that connects the two sides of the lake, dividing Kalamalka Lake from Woods Lake further to the south. Boats can go through a channel in the isthmus, underneath a bridge, to get into Woods Lake. We explored most of Kalamalka Lake. We would see cattle and occasionally cowboys on the beach at Cosens Bay, as this area was part of the Coldstream ranch. Once we talked to two cowboys that had stopped on the beach, and were warming up their coffee on a tiny little fire, a fire that barely seemed to be smoldering and yet must have been adequate for their purposes. It is the habit of many people to build a big roaring fire, but then this fire has to be put out as you move onward. The cowboys had solved the problem of getting the fire out, by keeping it no bigger than necessary.

As described earlier, one of our favourite spots was Jade Bay, to which my brother and I frequently rafted or boated. We went diving into the crystal clear bay, struggling to go down deep enough to touch the muddy bottom. Another favourite spot was a small bay close to the tip and on the east side of Turtle Head Point (frequently and incorrectly called Rattlesnake Point); our access to that area was primarily by water. Here there were two sloping rocks in the water which formed a natural anchorage to pull the

Figure 34 A favourite picnic spot near Turtle's Head point. One could dive from the rocks into very deep water. (VEM)

boat up, as the angle of the slope of the rocks matched the angle of the front end of the boat. This small bay was surrounded by tall cliffs and steeply sloping ground.

This was a fun place because there was numerous rocks that one could climb, and dive into the water which got very deep very quickly. Or one could climb the higher cliffs, and dive or jump into the water. We never saw any rattlesnakes, for which the area is famous, but once in climbing the cliff I found a rattlesnake skeleton with the rattle still attached. With the exception of this skeleton, I have never seen a rattlesnake on "Rattlesnake Point". We would leave the boat parked at this natural anchorage, and swim around the rocky and isolated shoreline of the point. We would climb the cliffs and leap off into the water, always narrowly missing the rocks in the water below

We occasionally saw crayfish at this bay on Turtle Head Point. Adjacent to the shore there were scattered large boulders, even though the water quickly became deep. The crayfish would emerge from underneath a rock, and crawl along the mossy surfaces of other underwater rocks. The slightest disturbance would frighten them away, and they would scamper back underneath a rock.

When I returned to live in Vernon in 2005, this area of Turtle Head Point had become a provincial park, with roadways and parking lots skirting the edge of the park. There was considerably higher usage of the whole point (which had been previously ranch land) and much higher usage of our favourite little bay, judging by the amount of litter and broken bottles. The higher level of waves due to the greater number of power boats left the water constantly wavy, which would make life hazardous for life under the rocks on the shoreline. I didn't see any crayfish, only beer bottles in the water.

Farther down the east side of the lake, there was another smaller point that had a similar natural place to pull a boat into the shoreline, between two sloping rocks. One of the Vernon doctors had started to build an unconventional cabin here, incorporating the features in the rocky hillside behind this area. All the building materials had to be hauled in by boat, as there was no road down this side of the lake (at this time). The doctor committed suicide before his dreams of building a house here were completed, and presumably the suicide had nothing to do with the construction difficulties. We never saw anybody at this site actually building anything. But there were many good places to dive off the rocks into the water from here.

One Saturday, a friend Michael and I were exploring far down

Figure 35 A home being built on the east side of Kalamalka Lake, at a location where there was boat access only. The home conformed to the natural flow of the rock walls. (VEM)

the east side of the lake in our boat. We saw a spot where somebody had had a picnic on the shore of the lake, and had gone away leaving the fire still smouldering. We pulled over and attempted to put the fire out. The only method we had of carrying water was the bailing bucket carried in the boat, which would only carry a couple of quarts (litres) of water at a time. We made many trips until we were absolutely sure that the fire was out.

The next morning, there was an enormous forest fire extending up the side of the mountain in a triangular shape, and the base of the triangle seemed to be at or near the spot where we thought we had put the fire out. There were immense billows of smoke, and one could see the burning forest under the smoke. The forestry service mobilized a great many men, and called in the fire-bombers, to put out a fire that we were sure that we had put out the previous day.

Aquatic and Shore Life .

I remember seeing large snakes (say, four inches (10 cm) in diameter, four feet (120 cm) long) at both Cosens bay and at the old Coldstream garbage dump. These were considerably larger than the garter snakes that we more commonly saw. My father called one a Bull snake, as we were originally afraid it was a rattlesnake. The dump was near to the (former) Legg property at the north-west end of the lake, and is now incorporated into the sageless "Sage Point" housing development. I imagine the snake at the dump ate the mice that devoured the food remnants; there were trees here so there must have been some water on this otherwise dry hillside.

My memories include standing quietly knee deep in the water, surrounded by very large schools of minnows. These schools would be six feet across and ten or so feet long; there must have been hundreds of fish in the schools. We could catch them in glass canning jars. The fish would come and nibble at the hairs on the legs, when I was standing still.

I'm not sure if these large schools of fish still exist. Of course the environment at the north end of the lake is considerably different now because of the increased density of power boats and the increased power of motors. The water in the lake is a dilute mud slurry in July and August, and it is impossible to see the bottom if the water is more than six inches deep. The schools of fish might still be there, but obscured. In September, the power boats go home from their summer vacation and by mid-September one can once again see the lake bottom. Kalamalka lake has regained its beauty.

I also remember timid common bullheads, or more correctly "miller's thumbs", hiding under the boulders, and darting out to capture a tasty morsel, then disappearing back under the rocks. They grew occasionally to a length of six to eight inches but more commonly were smaller, about three to four inches long. According to a fish book that we had in our house when I was young, they grow to be more than six feet long in salt water.

Does the miller's thumb still exist in Kalamalka Lake? Yes, although it is an endangered species in some US locations. In 1653, Izaak Walton wrote in the Compleant Angler about this unusual fish: *The Miller's-Thumb, or Bull-head, is a fish of no pleasing shape. He is by Gesner compared to the sea-toad-fish, for his similitude and shape. It has a head, big and flat, much greater than suitable to his body; a mouth very wide and usually gaping. He is without teeth, but his lips are very rough, much like to a file. He hath two fins near to his gills, which be roundish or crested; two fins also under the belly; two on the back; one below the vent; and the fin of his tail is round. Nature hath painted the body of this fish with whitish, blackish, brownish spots. They be usually full of eggs or spawn all the summer, I mean the females; and those eggs swell their vents almost into the form of a dug*. They begin to spawn about April, and, as I told you, spawn several months in the summer. And in the winter the minnow, and loach, and bull-head, dwell in the mud, as the eel doth, or we know not where; no more than we know where the cuckoo and swallow, and other half-year-birds, which first appear to us in April, spend their six cold, winter, melancholy months. This bull-head does usually dwell and hide himself in holes, or amongst stones, in clear water: and in very hot days will lie a long time very still, and sun himself, and will be easy to be seen upon any flat stone, or any gravel; at which time he will suffer an Angler to put a hook baited with a small worm, very near unto his very mouth: and he never refuses to bite, nor indeed to be caught with the worst of anglers. Mattiolus commends him much more for his taste and nourishment, than for his shape or beauty.*

Earning and Learning Experiences

Having fun on and under the lake was great, but we also had to pay our way. It was after the family moved to the lake that I was able to get my own paper route. Vernon at that time had only

---

* Archaic word for an udder.

a biweekly newspaper, which came out on Monday and Thursdays. A Kelowna newspaper made an attempt to penetrate the Vernon marketplace with a daily paper, and advertised for paperboys. This did involve a lot of work, since the paperboys first had to go door-to-door over their prescribed routes, and ask people if they would like to subscribe to the paper. The routes ended up with a few customers spread over what seemed like a great distance. It was Peter that first established the route. He remembers doing the route accompanied by our dog Smokey every day.

Once he was sixteen years old, he got a job at Safeway as a 'Courtesy Clerk' packing and carrying groceries out to the customers' cars. He would occasionally work in the evening following the store closing hours, stocking shelves. One of his fond memory was cycling home at 2 AM on vacant roads. He worked there until he left for University. I took over the Kelowna Courier route from Peter when he got the job at Safeway. The Kelowna Courier paper route was to a number of houses around the head of Kalamalka Lake, so I got familiar with many of the lakeshore roads and residences.

I had a Vernon News paper route that stretched between the town and the lake where we lived. This was an ideal route when school was in session. I would ride my bike to school in the morning, three miles away in the town of Vernon. Twice a week, after school, I and a dozen other boys would congregate at the Vernon News building where we would pick up the newspapers for our respective paper routes. Then I would ride over my route, dropping off papers at the various homes where the homeowners subscribed to the paper. My paper route largely followed the route that I would take to ride home in any case, although there were a couple of sidetracks up other roads. It didn't take all that much longer to ride home delivering newspapers as it did to ride home without delivering papers.

Once a month one had to do "collecting" and record keeping. This meant knocking on doors, and getting the money from the homeowners. Then the majority of the money was turned over to the newspaper, and a certain amount kept for the newsboy. Sometimes, the act of collecting meant going back to the house time and time again to catch people at home. Rarely at Christmas time was a tip given to the paper boy; it was much appreciated when this happened.

I first got this paper route when I was going to Junior High School, at the far side of Vernon. But I kept the round all through to the end of Grade Twelve. It was very easy to do, if I was riding my bike to school anyway, and it provided a bit, not an awful lot, of extra pocket money. I think some of the other kids felt that they had overgrown paper rounds, that delivering papers or even riding a bicycle was just "kid stuff", but I appreciated the money it made.

In the summer months, this meant a two-way trip to town to do the paper round, since I wasn't at school. The paper round did mean riding the bike to school in all weather, and I remember bundling up with scarves and gloves in the occasional cold spells. I think when the weather got really stormy, I had help from my mother or father in delivering the papers by car, as they drove home from work in town. But these were rare occasions.

A requirement for the paper delivery jobs was a bicycle. I was given a brand new Raleigh bicycle, as a gift from my parents, when I was in grade eight or nine. This was a three-speed bicycle (with gears inside the rear hub), and likely the best that one could buy in a small town like Vernon at that time. It came with complete instructions how to adjust it for maximum efficiency and take care of it. I took very good care of this bike, and learned how to change tubes and tires and adjust the gears. We rode our bikes everywhere. But I did want to lighten the pressure on the pedals, so Dad arranged to have a larger socket with a few more teeth installed, which lowered the gear ratio. In retro-respect, the need to lighten the pedal pressure is perhaps an indication of after-effects of the Polio which is described later.

I had a couple of jobs cutting and trimming lawns. One was

for a Mr. Burnham, who lived in the Kalavista subdivision across the lake from our home; his house was surrounded on three sides by the water of the Kalavista lagoon. This house was later referred to as "the log house on the lagoon". The second was for Dr. Duncan McCullough Black, the manager of the community Public Health Unit in which my mother worked for some time. The Blacks had a very large yard immediately adjacent to the lake, so there was a lot of mowing and trimming.

Dry-Land Boyhood Experiences

We lived in the Kalamalka Lake house while I attended all my junior and senior high school. An evening would commence with mother coming home from work and making dinner. The dinners were not notable, mother used to frequently mention that she was not a good cook, but she was certainly adequate for our needs. I used to dislike carrots, but mother and father insisted that I should eat them because of the vitamins and to develop night vision. So we used to frequently have mashed potatoes in which the carrots were mashed in with the potatoes so they were unavoidable.

After dinner, Peter and I would do the dishes, usually Peter washing and me drying. Later I was assigned the job of making sandwiches for the four children's lunches at school, so every night I made and packaged up sandwiches. The two young children used lunch buckets, but Peter and I took the lunch to school in brown paper bags; because of the cost of the bags, we brought the empty bags home again and used them repeatedly until they were too worn. I became very fed up with making sandwiches, and when I went to University I never made lunches. In those days, I had a good breakfast and had just a cup of coffee or two for lunch.

Dad brought home from his job at J.S.Galbraith & Sons long lists of columns of how the workmen spent their time, and Peter and I would add the rows and columns and make sure the two totals agreed. After dinner, we used to remain sitting at the dining room table and do these long sheets of additions. This was before the days of computers; Peter and I were the computers.

Afterwards Peter and I would disappear into our bedroom to do our homework or work on hobbies such as building model airplanes, ships, and cars.

Two of the first model aircraft that I build were the Gloster Meteor and the DeHaviland Vampire, the first jets built by the British Government after the invention of the jet engine. Father had seen one of these jets during the Second World War when his crew was flying a Lancaster bomber into Farnborough, the British aeronautical research center. He had secretly snapped a photograph of this strange aeroplane without a propellor, and was very proud of this photograph. The Gloster Meteor was the first model kit I was given as a present when a child, although I didn't appreciate the historical significance of the jet at the time. I also made a model of a Lancaster Bomber that my father had flown in, and a variety of other planes. Ships were much more complicated and required a lot more patience, but I did build models of the famous clipper ships Cutty Sark and the Flying Cloud. Peter moved fairly quickly from aeroplane models to models of cars, which he would modify and paint exotic colours. We both made balsa wood and tissue-paper aeroplanes, with the early ones powered by a rubber band. Peter moved onto motor driven aircraft, but didn't get as involved as the young fellow we had known at the other house.

In the evening, Mother and Dad would sit with their cups of tea on opposite ends of the couch, or Dad in his favourite La-Z-Boy chair and Mother with her legs extended on the couch. They would be quietly reading the newspapers or a book, occasionally exchanging a word or two. The image of Mother and Dad sitting quietly on the couch is a picture of contentment.

Our parents were always very supportive of our extra-curricular activities. Both Richard and Peter were in the Scouts, and Daphne was in the Brownies and Girl Guides. When we moved to the lake and got interested in boating, I took evening classes from the Canadian Power Squadron for three years. These classes taught one everything you had to know about managing a boat on inland waters.

All of the children took swimming lessons at the Kalamalka public beach, year after year. Daphne became certified as a swimming instructor. I never got beyond the Intermediate level, and didn't take the Senior classes, because each year the family would take holidays (as described later) at the end of the summer, and I would miss the exam year after year. But it didn't matter, I still learned how to swim, and still use swimming as a preferred exercise routine, as an adult.

At some point in these years, I took Saturday art classes from a local art teacher called Miss Jessie Topham Brown. She had a studio in town, adjacent to or near the highway through the city,

Figure 36 Peter and Vivian taking horse riding lessons.

and I believe I got there either by cycling or with Dad. It may be that Dad still worked the 44-hour work-week at that time, which included Saturday morning as I remember walking to Dad's work when my class was over. In time, however, the art became less interesting than lakeside activities, and I dropped out of these classes. I still have a linocut of a sailing ship dating from those classes. At that time, I was very enamoured of sailing ships, and would draw and doodle galleons charging through the waves, so it was natural that I applied these interests to her art classes. Miss Topham Brown became quite well known, she was honoured by being awarded the freedom of the city of Vernon in 1971. The largest gallery at the Vernon Public Art Gallery is named after her.

During one summer off school, we took riding lessons at Ms. Giles in the Coldstream. Ms. Giles seemed like an ancient old lady, and had an another ancient old lady living with her. I have no idea how old they really were, and what a young boy considers "ancient" has no reflection on their real age. Ms. Giles herself was of pioneer stock and there is a road named after their family. We must have been driven to the riding school on Saturday mornings, and sometimes walked back. The two ladies had some old gentle nags, and I was led around the yard on these sedate old horses.

Occasionally, our family used go on Sunday drives in the family automobile. We'd drive up Mount Revelstoke, or Silver Star Mountain, to the Adams River Salmon run, or explore some back roads such as that through Trinity Valley. We drove halfway over the Roger's Pass through the rugged Selkirk Mountains, before it was officially opened. This pass was named after Major A.B. Rogers, a surveyor who first found the pass through the mountains that made the trans-Canada rail route considerably shorter. There were pictures of us with enormous snowbanks beside the road. For these outings, mother would make a picnic lunch. A family favourite sandwich was what was called a "Dagwood sandwich", consisting of peanut butter, bananas, bologna, lettuce and possibly other salad components such as cucumber. When travelling north, a favourite stopping place was Kaye Falls, near the Eagle Pass halfway between Sicamous and Revelstoke, where we would eat our lunch in the shade beside the fast flowing stream.

We grew up in the days before down-hill skiing became popular; instead, we went tobogganing as a family. On a winter Sunday afternoon, we would all get into the car and drive out to a hill called "Mount Baldy" somewhere in the Coldstream. We and many other citizens would haul our toboggans to the top of the hill, and slide down, then give other family members a chance. I had a home-made "Indian Sweater" and Daphne had a

Figure 37 Mother walking up the hill with toboggans at Old Baldy. (JWM, Early 1960s)

black and white one that had been purchased. These show up in the many pictures and movies of these events, which were happy togetherness times. Mother was always a bit timid in going down the hill on the toboggan, but she did it.

In addition to these family events, there were neighbourhood events. The children used to take the toboggans up the hill behind our house, across the road and railway tracks. In addition to the toboggans, we used the hood (or "bonnet") from the first Nash, the one in which we had driven across Canada. The hood ornament had been removed. It took five or six or more boys to haul that heavy car hood up the hill, but once it was up there about ten youngsters could get on it. Because of the weight, it would get considerable speed in going down the hill. I remember going all the way down and hitting the fence that isolated the fields from the railway tracks. Sometimes the hood would spin around until the sharp back edge of the hood dug into the snow, and it would rapidly spin the opposite way while still going down the hill. This was tremendous fun, but took cooperation from a group of neighbourhood boys. I think all the tobogganing events ceased when Peter and I went away to University, as mother and Dad took up skiing. The hood was abandoned on the hillside, and remained there until the hill was torn apart and reshaped for a housing development in 2006.

During his high school years, my younger brother Richard had learned to ski, and had joined the ski patrol, before leaving Vernon for University. He was also an avid photographer, and did the photography for his Junior and Senior high school annuals. This involved darkroom work being done at the school.

Mother and father became avid square dancers. I remember as a youngster going to square dances at Vernon's old Scout Hall (now demolished), and playing on the second floor as a youngster while the dance was going on. After the dance there were "pot-luck" refreshments. My brother Peter and I took lessons for a while, but felt out of place with the mostly adult dancers. I remember the callers at the time were Les Boyer and Joe Card

Figure 38 Mother and Father dressed for square dancing, in the front room of the house by Kalamalka Lake.

(The "callers" called out the moves that the dancers would then execute). Joe Card was a young and dynamic caller who quickly became a favourite amongst the dancers; he died tragically young. Square dancing became a passion with mother and father, and they travelled around the Central Interior going to many different square dance clubs. At times, both mother and father were on the executive of the Square Dance club. They made many firm friends who were dancers. Although I didn't really get involved in dancing at this time, when I moved to Dayton Ohio as a thirty-year old, I took up square dancing again as a means of meeting people, and had many good times with the dancers in Dayton and Cincinnati.

The disadvantage of living at the lake, a few miles out of town, is that we were isolated from the friends that we had made at school, at least until we got old enough to drive. The school friends were just that, school friends, and not after-school friends. The houses immediately adjacent to us were summer cabins, not year-round houses, and only occupied a couple of months of the year. We did become friends with Billy (Peter's age) and Donny (my age) who lived a short distance away. But their interests were somewhat different from ours, and apart from sledding in the winter we didn't do many activities together. Peter and I grew up doing activities that we could do by ourselves - making models, reading, stamp collection - rather than taking part in team activities with friends. We always enjoyed and looked forward to the visits of our cousins from Salmon Arm, as Brian was intermediate in age between Peter and myself, and we seemed to have a lot in common.

Adventures in Ranching

My parents used to frequently buy meat in bulk, and keep it in the chest freezer until needed. They would typically buy a side of beef, and have it butchered to their specifications. One year they decided that they could feed the family at less cost by getting involved in the food chain even earlier; they bought young calves instead of slaughtered parts of a full-grown steer. They made an arrangement with friends (the Johnsons) to keep the two calves on their property until they were old enough to be slaughtered, and the Johnston family would keep one of the two calves. We must have split the work in feeding them, or maybe we only did the feeding when the Johnsons were out of town. There were numerous phone calls to our house that the cattle were loose, and wandering down the streets or through somebody else's field. Peter and I would have to cycle down there, locate the two young steers, and herd them back to the Johnson's farm, trying to avoid traffic all the way. They certainly seemed very ingenious at finding their way out of the fenced compound. In the winter, they had to be fed daily, and occasionally Peter and I had to do this when the Johnsons weren't available. This involved carrying a bale of hay from a hay stack over to the feeding troughs, breaking open the bale and spreading the hay out over the trough. The young steers shared the field with a couple of high spirited horses belonging to the Johnson girls. These were good horses in the sense that they never got out of the field even though the steers repeatedly got out of the same field. However, they made it known that they did not like the cows to be fed. While struggling across the field with a heavy bale of hay the horses would charge us, then veer away, or buck right next to me. Once I was gently kicked by one of the horses. I became much more afraid of the horses than of the cattle. There was a great feeling of relief when the time came for the cattle to be slaughtered, and my parents never got so adventuresome as to try this again.

Summer Vacations

Because we lived beside a lake, there was no point in taking a summer vacation at a cottage beside a lake, and we no longer used the cottages and lakeshore property described earlier. Instead, every year we did a family vacation together. One year it was to Michichi in Alberta, where Mother had some relations. On this trip, we visited the Hoodoos (geological features caused by rain and wind erosion) in the nearby badlands, and camped with the dinosaurs on St. George's Park in Calgary. That year we also visited Fort McLeod. When I was 16 years old, we went to Barkerville (but Peter didn't come along, it was more important that he work at Safeway). Another year it was Banff, which had a gondola lift taking tourists up to a viewpoint high up the mountain ... Daphne became very upset because she was afraid of heights and didn't want to go down the gondola lift. On one of the early years the destination was the Vancouver area; we walked over the suspension bridge at Capilano Canyon. We walked from the highway down to Hell's Gate to look at the rapids that blocked the Fraser River and the fish ladders that allowed migrating salmon to bypass the rapids. In later years a tramway was built to avoid that very steep walk.

Our longest trip was southwards, camping along the Oregon coast, going as far as northern California. On that trip there was six of us in the little Austin Mini-minor, with all the camping and cooking gear in a roof-top-carrier. How we all fit in this small car seems miraculous; we were all neatly packaged with no room to move. The first days we were intent on making a substantial start on the trip, so we could then travel more leisurely. Mother however became quite hysterical when Dad was steering our small heavily-laden car through the freeways near Portland Oregon. But what a vacation this was, and what memories it gave us! We climbed the big tower at Astoria, camped on the beach with our big canvas tent, survived vicious rainstorms, went rolling down the huge sand dunes, and went swimming in the big breakers of the Pacific Ocean. We drove the Mini in the sand along the beach, and explored the wrecks and the sea lion caves and the many assorted tourist traps. We stopped at Klamath in California, which had a huge statue of Paul Bunyan. I was disappointed that we didn't continue on to Eureka, the city whose radio station I had listened to so many times in the evenings. On this trip I used my savings to buy a transistorized radio that included a short wave band, but it wasn't as good as the old one beside my bed. My sister bought me a souvenir penknife as a birthday present which I still had many years later.

After the year of the Oregon trip, Peter and I had summer jobs and didn't go with the family on their annual vacation; making money for university was more important. Mother and Dad did repeat the Oregon trip, however, with Richard and Daphne.

All these holidays were completely recorded because of Dad's skills with a camera. In addition, many scenes were recorded on an 8-mm camera. The 8-mm camera produced films that were only three minutes long. Dad spent considerable time splicing the short films together to make longer films. We spent a number of evenings at home viewing these films. I remember that Dad would take pictures of Peter and me diving into the water. By playing the movies at slow motion, or playing them backwards, we could see the position of our legs as we hit the water, and strive to improve our diving posture. So his hobby became a teaching aid. Many of these movies were later preserved on a digital video disc recording.

JUNIOR HIGH SCHOOL - GRADES SEVEN TO NINE

This is the Junior High School that I attended at age 13 to 15 (Grades 7 to 9). This picture was taken considerably later (in 2017 by VEM); the front entrance to the school has been considerably changed.

I was attending a Junior High School that was later named for W.L. Seaton who was the vice-principal at the time I was a student. The school was located towards the north end of the city in the large green MacDonald Park. Our physical education classes were held here, and we occasionally played soccer here. But I seldom got involved in any extracurricular sports activities because of the distance to our home. I most often cycled to school.

As a boy I had the usual childhood diseases. About the most serious thing that happened to me was an attack of a parasite called "ringworm". This was treated with poultices, and eventually went away. For a while it restricted my swimming which was had a big impact on me. But in 1959, something much more serious was diagnosed. It was discovered that I had polio. I was treated by our family doctor Hugh Alexander, and later by a hot-shot young pediatrician fresh out of college. This gentleman was Dr. Art Sovereign who became one of Vernon's most respected citizens. It was suspected that I caught polio from the vaccine that was supposed to prevent the disease. The vaccine is a weakened form of the virus intended to stimulate the growth of antibodies for the virus. In my case, I suppose the virus wasn't weakened enough and I caught the disease. I was told that my infection was written up in medical journals.

I didn't know anything about polio, so it didn't worry me. But my infection caused panic in the older generation who were used to the polio epidemics of previous years, that left thousands of people in wheelchairs for the rest of their lives. There was no treatment except that I was put in an isolation ward for observation. The diagnosis was confirmed and followed by taking samples of the spinal fluid using a needle that passed between the individual bones of the vertebra. This was done weekly as a check up on the progress of the disease. But the disease didn't progress. After a while, I was no longer in isolation, but shared the room with another young patient. After forty days or so I was released from hospital, and after another couple of weeks at home regaining my strength I returned to my grade 7 class after an absence of eight weeks.

For some people, being in isolation for a long period of time may have been a terrible punishment, but I didn't find it too much of a strain. I did a huge number of jig-saw puzzles, so many that I have only done a very few since that time, and only when I'm coerced to for social reasons. I had been given a book on "How to Sketch", and I went through this in great detail. One example they gave was of cartoon figures, and I still draw these figures occasionally. But mother had the foresight to talk to my teacher and bring me some of my schoolbooks. I studied the books and in particular the mathematics book, and did a lot of the exercises. My parents were afraid that when I returned to school from the prolonged absence I would have a lot of catch-up work to do. But instead, I was at the head of the class. One book that I did not have was my history book, and when I returned to school I found that the students had studied Egyptian and Babylonian (or Persian) history and were now onto Greek history. I regretted missing that part of the history lessons.

At the junior high school, students had an option of taking either band or choral music, and I chose choral music because this saved the money to buy or rent an instrument. I remember listening in the class to the "Sorcerer's Apprentice", and singing "June is Busting out all over" (from the musical Oklahoma). However, when the time came for the year-end show for the parents, the teacher Mr. DeWolf said that I wasn't good enough to be in the show, that I "sang in my boots", and suggested that I be the stage manager.

Mr. DeWolf was said to be single, and drove a fancy white convertible, which was usually parked beside the street across from the school. Apparently (I didn't see this happen), one day a group of the students lifted or jacked up his car and put supports under his rear axle so the wheels didn't touch the ground. After school, Mr. DeWolf is alleged to have started his car, found that it wouldn't move (since in those days most cars including this one were powered through the rear wheels), stepped on the accelerator at which time the car fell off its supports and accelerated rapidly, running into the car that was parked in front of it. So the fancy white convertible was scarred!

In grade eight, I was having trouble spelling. It was arranged that I would have special after-school lessons with my teacher, who was a rather stern fellow called Mr. Inkster. I suppose this helped a bit. But in grade ten, by that time in a different school, I studied Latin. And somehow, maybe it was the study of Latin or maybe it was sheer perseverance, my spelling problems evaporated and in later years I felt quite proud of my ability to spell correctly. (I and a few of my friends took Latin in Grade XII as an alternative to French which would otherwise have been required).

While in this junior high school, I made friends with another boy named Stanley. We were both interested in Mathematics, triangular numbers, Fibonacci numbers, and other mathematical concepts. Stan had the idea that the "perfect" numbers could be found in Pascal's triangle. We did a lot of calculating trying to find out if this was true or not, in collaboration with the mathematics teacher, Mr. Seaton Jr, the son of the vice principal. At the school graduation at the end of grade nine, we were both awarded very good slide-rules which I used most of the way through University - this was prior to the age of portable computers or even hand calculators. Stanley went on to use his numerical skills as an actuary for a Life Insurance company, and later for the Workmen's Compensation Board.

THE HIGH SCHOOL YEARS

Clarence Fulton Senior Secondary School.

This school graced Polson Park, providing a wonderful environment for lunch time walks. It was built in 1937 and had a date with a wrecker crew a few short years after I attended in 1965.   (The picture is from an old high school annual, photographer unknown.)

These are the years in which boyhood and boyishness is left behind, and one starts to mature. I was handicapped by being extremely shy, and did not partake extensively in any high school activities. I attended Clarence Fulton Senior Secondary School, a three story concrete and brick building on the edge of Vernon's beautiful Polson Park. It has since been torn down, as Vernon has grown and there are now two newer schools but both in the suburbs, away from the town centre.

Although there was bus service from near our home to the school, our main method of transportation was the bicycle. Bicycle riders were also a minority, I don't think it was "cool", but I wasn't so concerned about being cool as in having the personal freedom to come and go as I pleased, apart from the necessity to attend classes. But maybe this also was part of being shy, I just didn't want to hang around and be in a situation where I would have to talk to people.

In hindsight, although I describe my shyness at some length, perhaps I wasn't any more or less shy than other boys my age.

Occasionally, however, we walked home from school, and the shortest walk was along the railway tracks as the tracks passed immediately behind my parents' house. This walk took us through the fearsome "Hobo Jungle", reputed to be occupied by homeless and nomadic people. I never once saw a hobo or a homeless person.

My father worked nearby, and if there were after-school activities, we could have ridden with him. But generally speaking his eight AM to five PM working hours were poorly timed coincidence with the nine AM to three-thirty PM school hours. In those days, only a small fraction of high school students owned their own cars, and the school had very little provision for student parking.

At a certain age, a young man's thoughts inevitably turn to love, long before he knows what the word means. Perhaps there is an instinct built into each one of us that wants the company and admiration of a member of the opposite sex. In my case I was madly in love with an astoundingly pretty young lady for most of my high school years. She was cute and petite and had her smart brown hair done up so nicely. For a couple of years she was in my home room, but it was only in Grade twelve that I was actually in a class with her. She sat in the front seat of a row of seats of the opposite side of the room, and I would daydream about being sauve and sophisticated and going up to her and making some smart comments and she would be mine forever and I would be the envy of all the other guys. She was the only one for me, and I was very faithful to her. But I didn't actually speak to her, not once in my three years of high school! I was far to shy to talk to her. In fact for the whole of my time in high school, I never said more than half a dozen words to a girl. Shyness is such a curse! At the same time I was highly envious of the boys who could open up and chat with girls.

I was involved in a "Ping-Pong" group at school, during lunch time and after school. The table-tennis tables were set up in the east cafeteria of the school. This was a guy's domain with very little intrusion of members of the opposite gender. They had the other main cafeteria. Cafeterias in those days did not need to be and were not supervised by a teacher, they were all in the teachers' staff room enjoying their lunch break, and we seldom saw a teacher in our east cafeteria. The ping-pong group was very informal, with no membership, people just dropped down and played.

The school was located in a beautiful park, called Polson Park, and we used to frequently walk around the park during lunchtime. There had been a large chequer board set in concrete in part of the park, with large painted wooden chequer pieces. A friend Stanley and I used to frequently play chequers at lunchtime. I had only been to Stanley's parents place once or twice, and I only invited him once or twice down to our place at the lake. We were best friends at school, but the friendship seemed to be limited to schooltime only.

Another friend was Michael. He and I were very competitive

for marks in school. We also both listened to distant radio stations in the evening, and would often compare notes the following day. When I got my driver's licence, I would occasionally drop around at his house in the evening and chat, but we didn't have an awful lot to do with each other. It was forty years later that I learned that Mike's father had died during our high school years. At that time Mike, with three sisters, was the head of the household. But this was not talked about, and I didn't know they were orphans.

It is said that most people in the world remember what they were doing when the President of the United States, John Kennedy, was assassinated in 1963. It was "Sadie Hawkins" day at our school, when most people dress up to emulate the characters in a newspaper comic strip. Although the comic strip has now disappeared, it was very popular at the time, and the practice of "Sadie Hawkins" day was very wide spread. So not wanting to be left out, we had dressed up. Then in mid-morning, the news of the assassination was broadcast over the school loud-speaker system. Thereafter periodic updates were announced. I and many of us felt very out of place, dressed up to have fun, and suddenly the fun was gone from the day[*].

I did take once a week evening classes through the local chapter of the Canadian Power Squadron, but this was not affiliated with the school. In successive years, I took their first boating class, called "Piloting", then their courses in "Seamanship" and "Advanced Piloting". The classes were held at the Vernon Yacht Club on Okanagan Lake. Rides were arranged for me with another member of the class, a retired Colonel Husband who lived in a mansion[**] in an orchard up the hill at the north end of Kalamalka Lake. I became quite attached to Colonel

---

[*] Other people that I went to school with have other recollections of the day that John Kennedy was shot.

[**] This is the only home in the Vernon area designed by the architect Rattenbury who also designed the provincial parliament buildings in Victoria.

Husband and his wife; their children had already left home, and they had quite a library of boys' books which I was encouraged to borrow. I remember in particular books by Horatio Alger and G.A. Henty, and the well-known Lowell Thomas book about Lawrence of Arabia. I thought it strange the Colonel Husband didn't know how old he was; he said he was born on the prairies where record keeping was very poor so there was no record of the date of his birth. Another gentleman I remember from the Power Squadron Classes was Jack Monk ... I called at his house a couple of times; he was a bachelor who had a pet parrot that had a wonderful command of the more colourful parts of the English language. I was the only student in a class of adult boat owners.

In addition to the summer jobs (described later) and the newspaper routes previously mentioned, I had a number of other jobs that provided pocket money during the high school years. I tutored in mathematics the son of one of the junior high school teachers; I don't know what marks he got as a result of my tutoring, but he must have at least passed. I also had some jobs baby sitting. One of the families that I babysat for was the Harley family. Norm Harley ran a fabric shop. His son, Dave Harley, whom I babysat as a young man, went to University but later started a manufacturing company "Far West" that made winter sports wear. Dave Harley was one of the chief clothing designers at Far West. In later years, Far West became a public company and any association with the founders was terminated; Dave then started a second company "Valhalla Equipment"

I have written this much about the high school years without actually mentioning school. My favourite subject was Mathematics. During grade eleven, a bunch of the more advanced boys including myself studied mathematics independently in the east cafeteria (the Ping Pong room) instead of attending regular classes. At the end of the school year, I not only wrote the grade eleven mathematics exam, but also the grade twelve exam, and passed them both. The next year I was in grade twelve; then I took the grade thirteen (first year University) course by correspondence, and started studying calculus. The physics course was very experimental – we used cars pulling tickertape going down different slopes, and measured the spaces between the marks on the ticker tape to calculate speed and acceleration, confirming the laws of mechanics. We also had wave-tanks to study waves action and interference between different waves. It was a very interesting way to learn. Chemistry was more conventional and much less interesting. I wrote a report on parasitic worms in Biology class. English was also very interesting, studying poetry and plays, although I wasn't very good at memorizing. Every year in English we studied a play by Shakespeare, with the parts spoken out by different students in the class. The Merchant of Venice, Julius Caesar, Romeo and Juliet were studied in different years. One year we had Robert Martin as an English teacher; he was very involved in the local theatre group, and put a lot of passion into his teaching.

I had taken shop (woodworking, drafting, and metalworking) in junior high school and didn't continue on with this in high school. I took an extra geography class that wasn't required; this was the geography of British Columbia. I wasn't very athletic, and the class I didn't like was Physical Education. For the first couple of years of high school athletics the teacher was Mike White, who had an easy-going teaching style. But then we had a Mr. Webster, a hot-shot just graduated from a college in the United States, and we all knew those American colleges considered athletics and football and basketball far more important than any book learning. Physical Education with Mr. Webster was up-and-down the bleachers, round and round the track, up-and-down the dirt slopes at the far end of Polson Park. It seemed that he was determined to make super athletes out of us, and some of us weren't meant to be super athletes.

Graduation inevitably occurs at the end of high school. There was a ceremony in the school gymnasium, followed by a party at the Country Club beside Kalamalka Lake. This was my very first date, the very first time I had to get close to a girl. I was tall and

Figure 41 Award of Canadian Legion scholarships at the end of grade 12, 1965. Left to right, a representative of the Vernon Branch of the Canadian Legion, Stanley Warawa, Evi Rosin, and Vivian Merchant. Vernon News Photograph.

thin and awkward and gangly. I probably had a reputation as a "geek" or a "nerd", although those terms weren't used in those days. Some of the high school boys had the nerve to ask their favourite girl out to high school graduation, but not me and some of my friends. One of the high school teachers paired us awkward guys up with young ladies that hadn't found partners. This same lady teacher also tried to teach us how to dance, but that was a lost cause.

The higher powers had decided that I was going to take a young lady called Roseanne* to the Graduation Party. Roseanne

---

* The name has been disguised to protect the
innocent.

was a somewhat shy girl, academically inclined, somewhat taller than many of the other girls. She had been in my classes for many years. I remember picking her up on that fateful night at her parents' house – it was the first time that I'd been there – in my parents' car. I think I had a corsage, but I had no idea what to do with it; she pinned it on her dress. I remember that she was dressed very smartly, but I totally forget what I was wearing. The graduation party was held at the Vernon Country Club on the shores of Kalamalka Lake; it was the first time I was ever in this building that I had driven by many times on my newspaper route. It was decorated very well but somehow I just felt out of place. The vivacious Roseanne and the very shy Vivian took in most of the party, then I drove her back to her parents' place and dropped her off and went home. I didn't know what else to do. Social graces were not my strong point at that stage in my life. In retrospect I felt sorry for Roseanne, she deserved a much more outgoing and "fun" person than the bashful and socially-inept me.

Cars and Other Activities

After I turned sixteen, I learned how to drive the family car. I took lessons sponsored by the high school, graduating in June of 1964 in time for summer jobs. In the last year of school however, I continued to ride my bicycle to school, since mother and dad needed the family car. This family car was an Austin "Mini" (or Mini-Minor), with a small 0.85 liter engine that powered the very lightweight car.

Peter and I occasionally had use of the family car on a Friday or Saturday evening, when we had money for gasoline. Generally speaking we didn't have anywhere to go to, with not a lot of extra money for outside activities. We would cruise around town, doing "mainers", a term which denotes driving back and forth along main street. The main purpose of doing mainers was to gawk[*] at

---

[*] The dictionary definition of "gawk" is "stare stupidly", which is appropriate.

the girls on the sidewalk, which I suppose is the first step in a primitive mating ritual. But it was a fruitless endeavour, as Vernon's girls had a lot better things to do with their time than to stand around on sidewalks and be gawked at. Gawking at young ladies for us was like a dog chasing after a car; the dog wouldn't know what to do with the car if it caught one. We shy guys wouldn't know what to say to a pretty young lady even if she had been magically transplanted to the car seat beside us.

I believe the term "we" refers to me accompanying my older brother Peter and his friends Tony and Don. This is not an activity that one would do alone, and I don't think I had any close friends at that time to gawk with - perhaps I went a time or two with Michael. But he was much more brazen, at one point he did a "mainer" with some of his other friends, with an hood ornament on the car made of plasticine and representing an erect penis. He didn't get arrested for this; likely nobody noticed.

After doing a couple of mainers, fruitlessly, we would frequently go to the drive-in theatre to watch a movie. But food was a requirement before the movies. The mainers would frequently take us through "The Dip", a popular restaurant near the top of Vernon's Mission hill. We didn't stop there, but went instead to the A&W drive-in, and order food. The reason for the A&W was that we didn't have to get out of the car; the order would be taken and delivered by a young lady wearing a short skirt, so eating at the A&W added to the gawk-time. I remember just about always getting the least expensive burger on the menu, because I was younger than the others and less sure of my finances with my limited jobs. We would get root beer in mugs and occasionally try and drive off with a mug, but also get a gallon of root beer to consume at the drive in theatre. This was an exciting Friday night in Vernon.

One Friday evening, there was nothing good at the movies in Vernon, and we decided to drive to Penticton, 70 miles (100 km) away at the far end of Okanagan lake. This was a very fast drive. The speedometer of the Austin Mini only went up to 80 miles per hour, but there was a blank spot after that before a post at approximately the 90-mile-per-hour position. It was not difficult to drive that car so that the speedometer needle was stuck against the post. The needle was stuck to the post most of the way to Penticton and back, with Peter driving. We slowed down for Kelowna, and a little bit for Rutland, but other than that pushed the car's tiny 0.85 liter engine to the limit. Once we got to Penticton, we found that the movie on at their theatre was not suitable, so we did a couple of "mainers" in Penticton and returned to Vernon. Another exciting Friday night.

The real excitement occurred the next day. Father was driving the car to go and do some Saturday work, and on turning a corner on the way to Vernon one of the rear wheels came off the car and went rolling ahead of him. He was able to pull the car to the side of the road, retrieve and replace the wheel, and continue on his way. Beyond any shadow of a doubt, if the wheel had come off the previous night when we were driving the car at excessive speeds there would have been a very serious accident. We never told father about our near miss.

On another occasion, I had driven the car down the dirt road to Cosen's bay on a Saturday. But on driving back, the bottom of the car struck the ground when I cleared the top of a hill, and a moment later the red "Oil Pressure" light on the dashboard of the car came on. I stopped the car immediately, and walking backwards found that I had smashed the oil pan on a rock that stuck up from the dirt road. I walked some distance to find an occupied house from which I could sheepishly phone my Father. He never cast blame but immediately corrected the situation. Somehow, he went to his place of work, borrowed a truck, and drove to where I was. We connected a tow line between the two vehicles, and with him driving the first vehicle and me the second, he pulled the dead vehicle to his place of work. In the next few days, the motor was removed from the car, and the oil pan removed. It was found that the price of a new oil pan was excessive, so an extra piston was bought. One of his workmates who was a welder melted down the aluminum piston and used it to patch the hole in the aluminum oil pan. The car was back on the road in no time.

Peter had always been more fascinated with cars than I was, and he obtained a very old Maxwell Chrysler with the intention of fixing it up. But the intentions never came to fruition, and the car became the property of a friend who had more workspace. He also bought an older model, an Austin Seven, and drove that for a number of years. We made some trips to the drive-in theatre in this car.

Learning to drive and having access to our parents' car was an important part of the growing-up phase. We had lived at the lake where there were few nearby people of our age, and so I had very little social interaction with other people, and simply didn't know how to behave in public. Once we had the car, we were no longer tied to staying home in the evening, and could go out and mix with other people our age. In Vernon at that time, however, there wasn't really any place to go and mix, especially for people such as myself with very little extra pocket money. The mixing took place primarily at the two homes of friends, Bob and Michael. Their homes were much like "drop-in" centres where anybody was welcome to just drop in and check out the action and lack of, and where there was much friendly cajoling about interactions with members of the opposite sex. I appreciate the welcome spirit that their parents provided. Throughout the university years when we came home from the big city for Christmas and other holidays, we would drop in at Bob's house to catch up on all our friends and their activities. Unfortunately, our own house never seemed to provide the same welcome to high school friends. This was perhaps a continuing handicap from living just a bit farther out of town, a little less convenient for friends to drop in.

One of my favourite memories was driving on Kalamalka Lake when it was frozen. This happened frequently in those years, but never now - possibly a consequence of climate change. People I have met had skated all the way from Vernon to Oyama, at the other end of the lake. The lake never froze to that extent when I lived there.

When the North end of the lake was solidly frozen, my brother and I would borrow the family car and drive to the ramp where (in the summer) boats were moved from automobile-drawn boat trailers into the water of the lake. When the water at the base of the ramp was frozen, one could drive down the ramp and end up on the ice. If the driver would try and accelerate rapidly, the wheels would spin on the ice and the car would go nowhere. The spinning of the wheels could be avoided by accelerating gently and continuously. It would take a minute or two to get up considerable speed on the ice.

The family car at this time was the Austin "mini" which had front wheel drive. When going fast in this car, the driver could pull on the hand brake which locked the rear wheels. This prevented the rear wheels from turning, so they would just slide on the ice. If the driver would simultaneously turn the steering wheel sharply one way or the other, the sliding rear wheels would move to the side of the front wheels, and the car would start rotating while simultaneously moving down the ice in a straight line. As dangerous as this spiralling motion might appear, it was perfectly safe because there was nothing out on the surface of the ice to hit. It didn't matter if the driver had control of the vehicle or not.

But amazingly, the driver could regain control. By releasing the hand brake at a time when the spinning car was facing forward, and turning the steering wheel so the front wheels were pointed into the direction that the car was spinning, and then accelerating gradually, the car would pull out of the skid and once again go in a straight line under the driver's control. We repeatedly did this, throwing the car into an uncontrollable spin, and recovering, and in that way learned how to drive on icy highways.

We never told our mother and father about these adventures with their car. Father would likely have joined us on the ice driving the car.

Summer Jobs

In the North Okanagan, the main industries were lumbering, farming, and tourism. As an unskilled schoolboy, it is perhaps natural that many of my first summer jobs were in the agricultural industries. One summer job was thinning apples. The local orchardists were proud of the quality of their produce, but this was achieved by thinning the apples of every tree in the early part of the growing season. Immature apples would appear with three to five apples appearing from every clump of blossoms. All except one had to be picked off and thrown on the ground. It was felt that if two apples grew together in close proximity, they would each have a flat side where they abutted each other. This flat side would make them less then the highest quality perfectly-round apples that the customers expected. So each blossom, each branch, of each tree had to pruned of any dangerous extra apples that could possibly affect the perfection of those that were allowed to survive. The workers moved tall fourteen foot (four and a quarter meters), three legged ladders from side to side, from tree to tree, over this collection of trees that extended for many acres. And it seemed as if the majority of the land in the north Okanagan was covered with these fruit trees. They were planted in rows, with rows separated by enough room for the farmer to drive the tractor between them. In each row, the trees were planted close enough together that the branches of adjacent trees slightly, partly overlapped. In the Okanagan, the natural vegetation seemed to be grasslands, with occasional trees such as Ponderosa pine that had deep roots and could survive in long hot summers. The orchards existed only because of irrigation, which consisted of long strings of metal pipes with occasional sprinklers. One of the jobs of the boys who worked on the orchards was to move these lengths of sprinkler pipe from row-to-row, so over the course of a week or so the whole orchard would be watered. The "thinners" didn't do this job, but could appreciate the benefits of the irrigation. Beneath the trees there was lush green grass growing a foot or more high, and a wonderful smell of fertile soil. In the absence of irrigation, there would have been sparse dry grass, sagebrush, and the occasional pine tree. Clearly the irrigation was essential for orcharding in the Okanagan.

We manipulated those tall awkward ladders from tree to tree, climbing as high as we dared, and throwing a lot of immature green apples, an inch (25 mm) in diameter or smaller, onto the ground beneath us. There was a bunch of us schoolboys, but there were also some professionals ... adults who could work twice or three times as fast as the schoolboys, never stopped to chat, and had very little to say to the collection of schoolboys. I suppose these were itinerant labourers who moved from farm to farm, from one part of the country to the next, where ever there was work to be done. But they didn't talk to us.

In that case we were paid by the hour ... I think it was $0.90 per hour. I remember in the late summer having a job picking cherries. In this case you weren't paid by the hour, but by how much you picked. The same three-legged orchard ladders were used. One climbed up the ladder with a big canvas bucket suspended by a strap around his or her neck. The canvas of the bag was sewn around a metal frame into a semicircular shape with rounded corners; a metal bottom was hinged to the metal frame. With one hand on the ladder, or an adjacent branch, the picker reached out, plucked the cherries from the branches of the tree, making sure the stalk stayed with the cherry and not on the branch, and put the cherries in the canvas bag. When he or she had picked all the cherries within reach from the ladder, he would climb down and move the ladder to a new location. When the bucket was either too full or too heavy , the picker would empty the bucket into wooden boxes. The wooden boxes were invariably called "apple boxes" because they were also used for apples when they became ripe. In spite of the name, they were used for a wide variety of fruits at different times of the year. They were about

20" long by 12" wide and 8" deep[*] and made of thin slats of wood[**]. When the apple boxes were full they were loaded onto the flat bed of a trailer hauled by tractors. The pickers were paid so much a box full, rather than by the hour. This got to be a problem for people such as myself, who would pick two, eat one, pick two, eat one. This would not only cheat the farmer of the full value of the product that he had grown, but also cheat the picker out of a significant fraction of his earning potential. I think I only picked cherries for one season, and was usually back in school when apples became ripe.

One of my favourite high school teachers was John Baumbrough, who taught biology and chemistry. He was a large man, who seemed cheerful most of the time and was pleasant to be around. He had a farm on the outskirts of Vernon, on which he grew experimental seed corn. At the end of the season, the corn was collected, the seeds separated, and sold to farms where it would be grown into a real crop. Every fall, a collection of students would gather at his farm to gather in the corn. We'd go up and down the rows of corn, taking the corn off the stems and putting them in gunny sacks. Later we'd gather in a circle, and strip all the leaves off the ears of corn. John would then load all the ears of corn into a large machine, that would churn and grind away... the kernels of corn would come out one chute of the machine, and the cores were ejected out of another. This was not a long term job, as he didn't have acres of corn, occupying a couple of Saturdays only. It was a fun time period with people of my own age. I remember the friendship and fun that we had with John, his wife, and family and my friends who were also there helping.

---

[*] Approximately 50 x 30 x 20 cm

[**] More recently, the use of "apple" boxes has been replaced by much larger boxes made of thicker wood, which can only by handled by mechanized fork lifts.

Another job I had was helping to bale hay. At that time, the farmer used a hay baler that produced rectangular blocks of hay, about 1 foot by 16 inches by 3 feet*. They were bound in that shape using coarse baler twine. The hay was dry at the time it was baled, but it still had considerable moisture content and the bales were relatively heavy, about a hundred pounds (40 kg). It was important that the bales, which lay all over the field where ever the tractor-drawn baling machine dropped them, be collected up and put into a barn, or a large tarpaulin-covered stack, to be kept dry. If they became wet in a rain shower, they would never dry and likely rot, causing sickness in the animals to which they were fed. Ranchers generally needed one bale of hay per animal (cow or horse) for every day that the animals couldn't graze due to snow cover, and in some cases they were provided extra food in the form of the hay even when they were grazing, since the grass was poor in the winter and early spring.

To gather the hay, a tractor would draw a flat-bed trailer up to the hay bales scattered all over the field. A team of boys and men would throw the bales onto the trailer, where another couple of guys would stack them. I was one of the boys throwing these hundred-pound bales up to the trailer. As the trailer came completely covered with hay, and it was getting stacked higher and higher, this would mean throwing the bales a considerable distance up into the air. One quickly gained an appreciation for the hard work that farmers put into their livelihood. I think I only did this once, and it must have been to help out a family friend. I don't remember getting paid.

The summer after I completed grade eleven, I had a full-time job working at the Ice Plant. The Ice Plant was adjacent to the ice arena, and also adjacent to a railway siding. The building smelt of ammonia from leaking pipes, as ammonia was used as the refrigerant. It was before the days of refrigerated rail cars, and to

---

* Dimensions are from old memories, not from measurements, and are not necessarily accurate. This is approximately 30 x 40 x 90 cm.

keep produce at a cold temperature while it was being shipped, the cars were loaded with blocks of ice insulated with sawdust. The produce being shipped also fit into the box cars. The blocks[*] of ice were about 12 by 24 by 48 inches. The job involved moving around these heavy blocks of ice, for the whole summer. As the blocks were produced, they had to be manoeuvred and stacked in an orderly fashion. Then when a train came in, they were pulled out of the orderly fashioned stacks and brought over to where the experienced hands manipulated them onto the box cars. The blocks were grabbed with long cast iron tongs that closed around and gripped the blocks on both sides. I wore cleats that buckled over my boots and that had a bunch of sharp points that provided a grip on the ice. Using these cleats on my feet and tongs in the hands, I pulled each ice block over the layers and bunches of iceblocks underneath.

This was a wonderful job because it was cool. Vernon would get very hot in the summer; temperatures in excess of 100F (37C) were not uncommon and 110 (43C) recorded occasionally. But I went to work taking a winter coat with me, because I was working where it was cold.

I had this job after grade eleven, at which time I had my driver's licence; I drove the family's Austin Mini to the workplace. I dropped Dad off at his place of work, and picked him up after work, since the location of his work was on my way to work.

After grade twelve, I didn't get the summer job at the Ice Plant again. I remember going to work picking beans. What an awful job this was! These were bush beans, not pole beans, so the job meant crunching over the whole time. The taller one is, the farther it is to crouch, and I was very tall! The bean fields, which seemed to stretch as far as the eye could see, were out in the hot blazing sun. I was driven there in the morning with my older

---

[*] Dimensions are from old memories, not from measurements. Approximately 30 x 60 x120 cm

brother Peter, and I think we only lasted a day and a half before we walked off the job and walked the several miles home. Our careers were not to be in the bean-picking line-of-work.

After having giving up this job, I was constantly looking for another job, urged on by my mother. While it lasted, I spent some time thinning apples. About a half mile from our home was a plant of the British Columbia Hydro and Power Authority, commonly known as "B.C. Hydro". This outfit was a government-owned corporation responsible for the production and distribution of electrical power within the province. The majority of the power was hydro-electric, hence the designation "hydro" in the name. I had applied for a job there and during the time period following the termination of my bean picking career, I bothered the employment officer Mr Richardson incessantly about the possibility of employment. The concentration of effort on this particular job opportunity stemmed partly from the closeness of the BC Hydro facility to our home, partly from the urging of my mother, and partly because of the lack of other opportunities. But it finally paid off.

One day I was called to Mr. Richardson's office and told I had a job in the distribution department. The distribution department was responsible for distributing the power to individual homes and offices, and measuring the amount of power used at each location. My job for the last month of the summer was to be in salvaging and destroying old house meters.

Each house has a meter that measures how much electricity is used in the house, to provide the basis for the monthly power bill. The meters used at that time were encased in glass and sealed so the homeowner didn't have access to it. A small transformer caused a light weight wheel, mounted on precision jeweled bearings, to spin. The number of revolutions was counted and resulted in a charge for the amount of electricity usage. However, the current style of meter had been replaced by a newer style. Gradually the older style was removed from the houses of consumers of electricity, and stacked in a warehouse at the back of the BC Hydro facilities. My summer job was to dismantle these old house-meters, salvage the glass cover jars, since they could be reused on the newer style of meter, remove the jewelled bearings from some of the meters to build up an inventory of spare parts, remove a few of other components of the meter, and smash the remaining part of the mechanism so it could never be used again.

As I mentioned above, the Okanagan valley is subjected to extremely high temperatures in the summer. The BC Hydro plant I was hired from was a thin building, not protected by trees, that baked in the heat of the sun for the entire day. This was before the days when air conditioning was considered a necessity, and when it was very rare. This building was very hot to work in, and indeed anywhere in the outside world was hot to work in an Okanagan summer.

But I didn't work in this building. I worked in the storage shed to the back of the main building, the storage shed where all the old house-meters had been stored. This storage shed was largely underground, and although the roof received a lot of heat from the sun, the temperature of the shed was influenced by the cool earth surrounding it. So I spent the rest of this summer away from the heat of the sun, using a sledge hammer to smash old house-meters.

Another task I undertook for BC Hydro was a survey of an "Indian" Reserve. I'm not sure if this task was after grade 11 (1964) or after grade 12 (1965). At this time, virtually all the houses in town had electricity supplied to the house so the occupants had use of electrical appliances and lights. By contrast, the houses on the more isolated Reserve did not have electricity supplied at this time.

The "Reserves" are plots of land granted to the aboriginal inhabitants of the land when it was invaded (starting about 1600AD) by a large number of foreigners from overseas seeking a better life than they would have had in Europe and Asia. The newcomers brought with them the concept of "land ownership", and they granted the original occupants the use of restricted areas of life to pursue their traditional way of life of hunting, fishing and gathering. However, the first nations people[*] realized their traditional way of life was no longer suitable (partially due to over-hunting) and had taken up farming and ranching, but also sought employment in logging and other off-reserve industries[**].

My job was to go from house to house on the reserve, and to ask the occupants if they would use electricity if it was provided. At the time of writing many years later, I forget the details of the provision, whether the electrical company would supply power to individual houses or only along the main road to the property line, with the occupants responsible for power poles and wiring to go from the road to the houses. I passed the results of my survey on to my managers, and that was the end of it for me. With hindsight, it is surprising that I, a shy high school student, was asked to do this job. Perhaps I was doing this job, rather than a more senior person, as a sign of the lack of emphasis that the local authorities placed on this job.

---

[*] Commonly and incorrectly called "Indians". Nation - congeries of people of common descent, language, history, etc., inhabiting a territory bounded by defined limits (The Consise Oxford Dictionary).

[**] This two sentence account does not do justice to the history of the interaction between the original inhabitants and the new comers. Further reading is recommended.

LOOKING TO THE FUTURE

I entered my last year of high school on the "University Program", on the expectation of continuing on to University. The alternative was the "General Program", for students intending to go into the trades; this program required a slightly fewer number

Figure 42 Vivian, age likely 17, preparing for an interview for the Officer Training Plan. I am standing in front of the series of walls that were painstakingly built to stabilize the sloping bank and provide garden space. (JWM)

of courses completed for graduation (perhaps to allow for work experience or apprenticeship.) I think at home it had always been assumed that we would go on to college or University; I don't think other possibilities were ever even discussed. One of the locations that I was considering applying for was Mount Royal College in Calgary, which would have provided a program in Electronics technology.

The last year of high school was the time in which applications had to be made. For the residents in a relatively small town such as Vernon, going to University meant leaving Vernon and living in a big city. Within the province of British Columbia, the choices had been the University of British Columbia (in Vancouver), the University of Victoria, and the military colleges.

The government of Canada had (and still has) an ROTP (Regular Officer Training Plan) in which selected candidates are provided a university education in return to a commitment to serve in the armed forces for a number of years. The people chosen would graduate from the college as an officer in the armed forces. The University Education could be taken at military colleges such as Royal Roads in British Columbia or the Royal Military College in Kingston Ontario, or at some universities such as UBC in which the students would take regular courses but have military training in evenings, but be provided a living allowance.

Because the family was so short of money, Peter and I were encouraged to try for the Officer training plan. We had photographs taken and the extensive application forms were filled in. Both Peter and I were selected for further interviews, and had an expense-paid trip to Vancouver. This was likely our first time away from home without our parents. There was a day long set of interviews and testing - our first experience with psychological testing. Somewhat later we both heard that we were rejected from the program. In my case I was nominally rejected because of my eyesight.

By contrast, our cousin Brian was accepted under the officer training program. He went to UBC for engineering courses, and took the military training for one night a year. He however did not complete the program. A friend from high school, Bob, also was a successful candidate. He went to the College Militaire Royale at St. Jean near Montreal for two years and to the Royal Military College in Kingston for a further year. After graduation, he became a navy officer. Later he went for a double Master's degree in Engineering and in Marine Architecture at the Massachusetts Institute of Oceanography in Boston. As a result, he had a further commitment to serve in the Canadian Military.

Since my brother and I were rejected from the officer training program, we looked elsewhere for our education. At that time, the government of British Columbia was building a new University in the city of Burnaby. The new university was to handle the expected burst of students resulting from the "baby boom" following the Second World War. The press covered the construction of the University and the expected staffing with highly qualified professors. The excitement about this new university led to my applying to this school, and my application was successful. My marks were sufficiently good that I was awarded a Government scholarship. In addition, I received a Canadian Legion scholarship upon graduation from high school, and a scholarship from the Masonic organization in the province of British Columbia.

Having been accepted at Simon Fraser University, received the various scholarships, and with my summer job at BC Hydro and Power Authority, the next step in my life beckoned. This next step is described in the sequel to this book, *The Early Years at Simon Fraser University, A Student's History.*

CONCLUSION

The Parent's Conclusion:

My parents migrated to Canada in 1952. They were part of a much greater mass of postwar emigration, and their English backgrounds were not really suited for life in a rural agricultural community. My mother and father struggled financially for the first few years, before being able to afford a house, and my mother in particular resented the move from England.

They had their own home in a very beautiful part of the world and were well on their way to a retirement that would see them travel extensively to many countries. Within eight years of moving to Canada they were able to buy this house by the lake. Although it had been a "handyman's special" our father spent a lot of time changing the furnace from coal to oil and then to gas burning, installing a heating system, building bedrooms, fixing up the septic tank, putting in a lawn, and turning a steep brush covered bank into a terraced garden. The house became the envy of many of their friends.

At this point, they can be regarded as "successful" in the sense of being well-regarded members of the community. My father was involved in a number of organizations. They were successful in the community, successful financially, and had successfully raised four children to the point where they could pursue their own education and careers.

The Children's Conclusion

There is no conclusion to this story. For me, I am graduated from school, a young adult but still in so many ways a youngster. The next stage in growing up took place at the University, in the big city. At this point, however, I had all the skills to enter into this new world and build our own successes.

CPSIA information can be obtained
at www.ICGtesting.com
Printed in the USA
LVOW11s1432121117
556010LV00001B/87/P